ALABAMA
ARCHITECTURE

LOOKING AT
BUILDING
AND PLACE

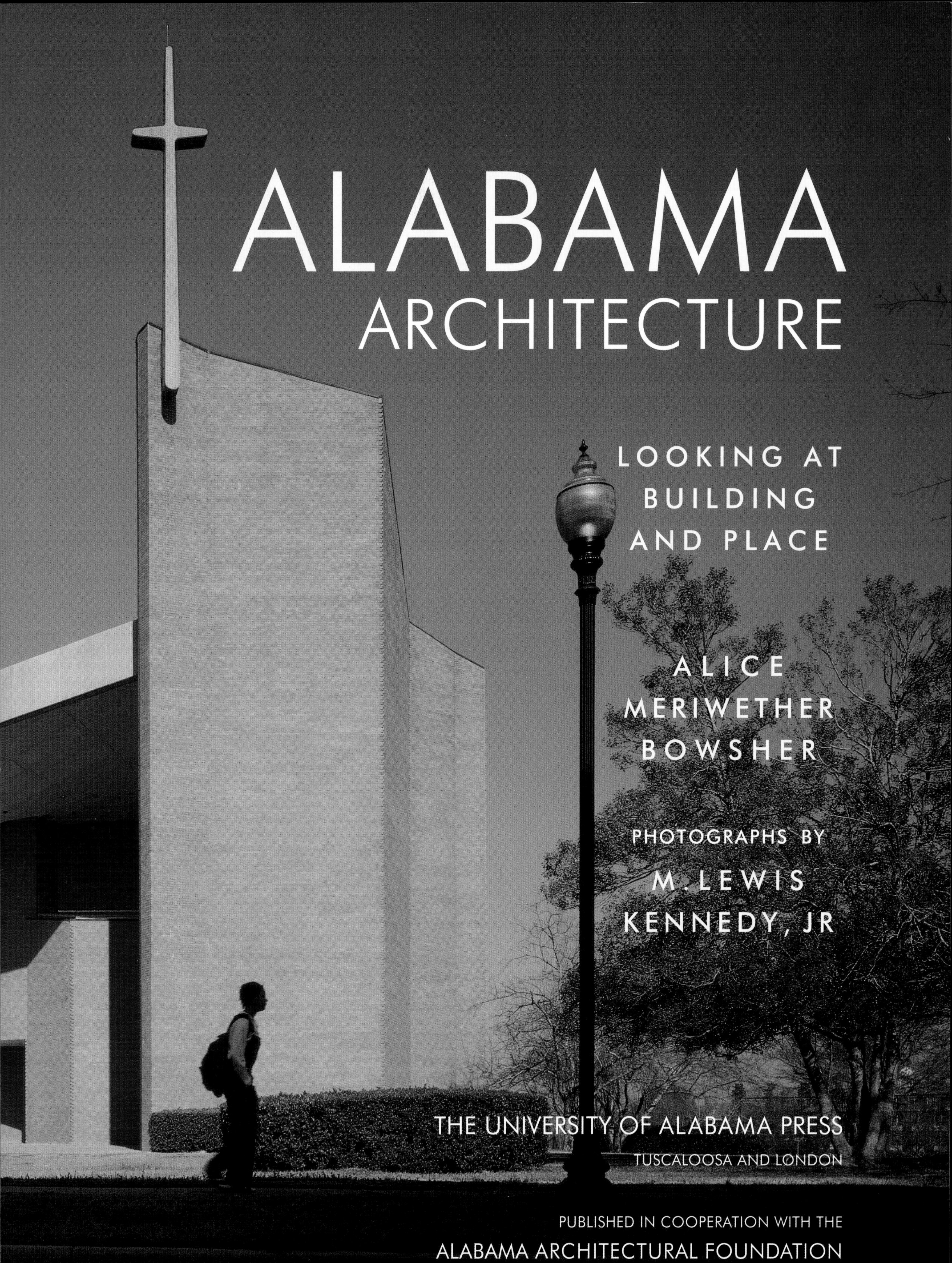

ALABAMA
ARCHITECTURE

LOOKING AT
BUILDING
AND PLACE

ALICE
MERIWETHER
BOWSHER

PHOTOGRAPHS BY

M. LEWIS
KENNEDY, JR

THE UNIVERSITY OF ALABAMA PRESS

TUSCALOOSA AND LONDON

PUBLISHED IN COOPERATION WITH THE
ALABAMA ARCHITECTURAL FOUNDATION

2 4 6 8 9 7 5 3 1
00 02 04 06 08 07 06 05 03 01

Designed by Robin McDonald

Typeset in Futura and Berkeley Oldstyle

The paper on which this book is printed meets the minimum requirements of
American National Standard for Information Science-Permanence of Paper for
Printed Library Materials, ANSI Z39.48-1984.

Portions of this project have been funded by the Alabama Historical Commission. Unlawful discrimination in this project on the basis of race, color, national
origin, age or disability is strictly prohibited.
Photography for this project has been made possible in part by grants from the
Alabama State Council on the Arts and the National Endowment for the Arts.

Excerpt from "Little Gidding" in FOUR QUARTETS, copyright 1942 by T. S.
Eliot and renewed 1970 by Esme Valerie Eliot, reprinted by permission of Harcourt,
Inc. and by permission of Faber and Faber.

Library of Congress Cataloging-in-Publication Data

Bowsher, Alice Meriwether.
   Alabama architecture : looking at building and place / text by Alice
Meriwether Bowsher ; photographs by M. Lewis Kennedy, Jr.
      p. cm.
"Published in cooperation with the Alabama Architectural Foundation."
Includes bibliographical references and index.
   ISBN 0-8173-1081-9 (cloth : alk. paper)
   1. Architecture—Alabama. 2. Historic buildings—Alabama. I.
Kennedy, M. Lewis. II. Title.
   NA730.A2 B69 2001
   720'.9761—dc21
                        00-011807

British Library Cataloguing-in-Publication Data available
Please see page 217 for identification of photographs on pages i–xiv and 1–3.

CONTENTS

FOREWORD

SINCE ITS INCEPTION IN 1983, the Alabama Architectural Foundation has pursued the goal of seeking ways to inform the public and make them more aware of architecture and of how good design affects each of us in our daily lives. We have awarded scholarships for excellence in design to students majoring in art and architecture, sponsored lectures and exhibits, and cosponsored an Alabama Public Television program on the Rosenbaum residence designed by Frank Lloyd Wright. Our audience has been limited, but the need has been compelling: to inform and excite the public about the value of architecture in Alabama. Thus the idea of a book to illustrate those buildings and places that have influenced our lives by their purpose and design seemed to be the most direct route to reach a larger public audience.

This project would have floundered if not for the directness, sensitivity, and love of architecture that Alice Meriwether Bowsher brought to it as the editorial director. She sought out, collected, analyzed, and selected from hundreds of sites around the state the finest examples of architecture to best represent the different aspects of architectural beauty within the state. Working with Alice, Lewis Kennedy completed the dynamic duo with his photography, presenting colorful and detailed portraits of these structures that grace the landscape of Alabama.

We express our gratitude to The University of Alabama Press for their commitment to participate in this endeavor. Without their engagement in the financial obligations to undertake the publishing and marketing, this book would not be available for several years.

The AAF Board of Directors deserves commendation, for without their patience and understanding, this project could not have been undertaken. The road was not always smooth, and it seemed to have nothing but hills to climb. We were at times unsure that there was a hilltop. Now we may not be at a pinnacle, but we are in a position to see where we are and to enjoy the view, feeling confident about our mission, for *Alabama Architecture: Looking at Building and Place* will soon be in the public's hands. It is important that all Board Members be thanked for their work and contribution: Evelyn Allen, Birmingham; Richard Barrow, FAIA, Birmingham; David Boozer, AIA, Anniston; Pat Conrad, Birmingham; Kimberly E. Harden, AIA, Montgomery; Major Holland, FAIA, Tuskegee; Renis Jones, FAIA, Montgomery; Lloyd Kranert, AIA, Huntsville; Don Lambert, AIA, Florence; Clark Lundell, AIA, Auburn University; Charles A. Moss, Jr., AIA, Birmingham; Dr. Sydney Spain, AIA, Auburn University; Ronnie Taylor, AIA, Mobile; and Scott Williams, AIA, Montgomery.

The Alabama Architectural Foundation is extremely grateful for the many who supported the vision of this book and the importance of getting it into the hands of the public. We are most appreciative to the Alabama Council of The American Institute of Architects for their contribution of a substantial start-up amount and the corpus of a larger amount as the substance of our growth.

— *Charles A. Moss, Jr.*
Alabama Architectural Foundation

D O N O R S

THIS PROJECT COULD NOT HAVE BEEN ACHIEVED without the generous support of those listed below, demonstrating their interest in and appreciation for our state and the architectural beauty that surrounds us:

Special Gift
Alabama Council of The American Institute of Architects

Foundation Grants
The Sybil H. Smith Charitable Trust
The Community Foundation of Greater Birmingham
Alabama Historical Commission
Alabama State Council on the Arts
BE&K, Inc., Birmingham
Gillian and Mike Goodrich, Birmingham
Susan Mott Webb Charitable Trust
Protective Life Insurance Foundation

Benefactors
ArchitectureWorks, Birmingham
Brasfield & Gorrie, LLC, Birmingham
Giattina Fisher Aycock Architects, Inc., Birmingham
Gresham Smith & Partners, Birmingham
KPS Group, Inc., Birmingham
J. F. Day & Company, Birmingham
Mobile Chapter, AIA
Sherlock, Smith & Adams, Inc., Montgomery
The Robins & Morton Group, Birmingham

Sponsors
Barter & Associates, Inc., Structural Engineers, Mobile
Birchfield Penuel & Associates, Birmingham
Houston and Betty Brice, Birmingham
Carapace Corporation, Birmingham

Crawford McWilliams Hatcher Architects, Birmingham

DuPont Corian™ Division, Wilmington, Delaware

The Garrison-Barrett Group, Inc., Birmingham

Goodrum Knowles, Inc., Huntsville

HKW Associates, P.C., Birmingham

Holmes & Holmes, Architects, Mobile

Jenkins Brick Company, Montgomery

JH Partners Architecture and Interiors, Huntsville

Lambert Ezell Architects, Florence

Lane Bishop York Delahay, Inc., Consulting Structural Engineers, Birmingham

Miller & Weaver, Inc., Consulting Engineers, Birmingham

Moss & Associates Architects, Inc., Birmingham

SKT Architects, P.C., Huntsville

Sloss Real Estate Group, Inc., Birmingham

SouthTrust Bank, Birmingham

Stallings & Sons, General Contractors, Montgomery

Stone Building Company, Inc., Birmingham

TAG/The Architects Group, Inc., Mobile

Evan Terry Associates, P.C., Architects, Birmingham

Turner Construction Company, Anniston

Friends

Architecture & Design, Inc., Mobile

Richard E. Barrow–Architect, Inc., Birmingham

Boral Bricks, Inc., Birmingham

CDC Engineers, Mobile

Pat Conrad, Birmingham

Cook's Pest Control, Huntsville

Covington Flooring Company, Inc., Birmingham

Cummings Architecture Corporation, Mobile

Walter H. Hopkins Company, Birmingham

Julian Jenkins, Architect, Anniston

Henry Sprott Long & Associates, Inc., Architects, Birmingham

Mayer Electric Supply Company, Inc., Birmingham

Jackie R. McCracken, Architect, Mobile

Patricia E. Sherman, Architect, Gadsden

SouthTrust Bank, Huntsville

In memory of Mary Crawford Meriwether

P R E F A C E

ONE OF THE GREAT JOYS OF GROWING UP in a Birmingham suburb in the 1950s was the freedom to wander and explore. My brother and I, along with neighborhood playmates, loved to make our way through houses under construction, after the workers had gone for the day, smelling fresh-cut wood and imagining what the partly framed spaces would become. Even more fun was venturing into the woods that were only a bicycle ride away, finding great rock outcroppings and creeks and adventure in the unknown. I have approached this book in a similar vein, in search of wonderful places down familiar roads and off the beaten track. It is written in hopes that both general readers and professional designers and historians will enjoy a sense of discovery, as you take a fresh look at Alabama and its architecture.

Methodology

At the beginning of this undertaking, the Alabama Architectural Foundation (AAF) invited chapters of the American Institute of Architects (AIA) to nominate buildings for inclusion in the book. This was followed by a similar invitation to more than seven hundred individual members of the Alabama Council of the AIA, as well as other designers, art and architectural historians, urban designers, and historic preservationists.

In selecting the buildings, architectural significance was a primary consideration, coupled with a desire for some surprises—buildings notable but not so well known. Since it is a book of photography, visual impact and variety were also important. And there was the need to fit each building into one of the abstract concepts that make up the chapters of the book—a fun and sometimes challenging exercise in seeing with understanding and imagination. Finally, an effort was made to represent all regions of the state, all periods, and a wide range of building types and styles.

The distribution, however, is not perfect. There are more buildings from the Birmingham and Mobile areas, reflecting in part their wealth of resources as the state's leading cities. Some other regions of the state with noteworthy buildings are underrepresented. There are more buildings from the late nineteenth and twentieth centuries because there are so many of them with merit and because the antebellum period has traditionally received more attention. Of course, the choices also reflect my personal enthusiasms. Although many people provided information and expertise, the decisions ultimately were mine alone. I am grateful to the AAF Board of Directors for giving me the freedom to make selections with complete independence, and I take full responsibility for the choices I made. Unfortunately, many worthy buildings from all areas of the state had to be omitted because of the limits of time and budget.

For the captions and building credits, likewise, numerous people generously provided information and insight, but I am responsible for their final content and accuracy, as I am for the chapter introductions.

A Note on Sources

In the interest of readability, I have omitted footnotes. Sources cited in the Introduction and in the body of each chapter are listed in the Sources/Bibliography section of the book. All works and authors cited in the captions appear in the Bibliography.

A Note on Building Information

Names in parentheses are historical names. In the instances when a building or place continues to be best known by its historical name, that is the only name used.

Years given are the date of construction.

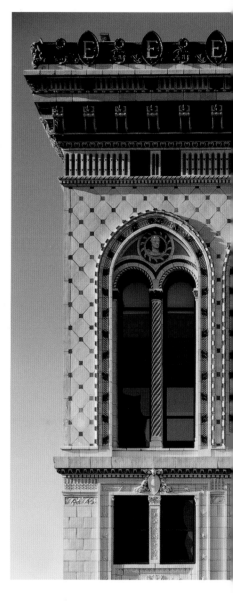

The term "master builder" is used to recognize the role of skilled artisans in the design of buildings through the mid-nineteenth century. Until the establishment of architecture schools in the United States later in the century, most buildings were designed by skilled carpenters or masons who had learned the art of building design through their trades, sometimes assisted by handbooks with architectural details. Many fewer buildings were designed by gentlemen amateurs or by full-time architects who had theoretical as well as practical training and who provided design but not construction services.

The term "builder" usually indicates the person who is credited with construction. "Contractor" usually means the "general contractor" or company that has overall responsibility for the construction work, including the work of the subcontractors.

Dates and architect and contractor credits generally refer to what is shown in the photograph. For parts of the building not pictured, specific information is usually omitted.

Only when the architect or contractor is from out of state is a city or state given.

The current names of architectural firms and contractors are generally used, even though they may have been operating under a different name at the time of the project.

NHL indicates recognition as a National Historic Landmark. NR indicates listing in the National Register of Historic Places, either individually or as part of a National Register historic district.

Every attempt has been made to obtain complete and accurate information, but there will inevitably be corrections and additions as new material comes to light. I welcome new information, with appropriate documentation.

— *Alice Meriwether Bowsher*

ACKNOWLEDGMENTS

MANY PEOPLE HAD A HAND IN BRINGING this book to fruition. Without Charles Moss's unrelenting desire to publish a book on Alabama architecture and the support he garnered from the Alabama Architectural Foundation, the project would not have happened. Without the creativity and talent of photographer Lewis Kennedy and designer Robin McDonald, my collaborators *par excellence,* the project would not be all that it is. Bobby Frese and Diane Maddex provided publishing insights, ideas, and encouragement as I was developing the early concept of the book, and Ellen Elsas provided able grants assistance. Once I plunged into the writing, Marvin Housworth took time out from designing buildings to have several conversations that helped expand and sharpen my thinking about the architectural ideas presented in the chapters. I also drew on years of exchanges with Gray Plosser about design. At every stage of the project, from the time it was only a glint in Charles Moss's eye to the invaluable reading of final drafts, Robert Gamble and Ellen Mertins of the Alabama Historical Commission provided an indispensable statewide overview and great insight and depth of knowledge about Alabama architecture.

The nitty gritty of logistics is essential in achieving the finished product, and we were fortunate to have the help of several people in coordinating scheduling and scouting and general troubleshooting. Wynter Byrd stepped in at a critical time in the photography schedule and gave it her full energetic attention to help us reach completion. Others who played important roles handling assorted details during the course of the project were Pam Short, Lisa Bunting, Susan Atkinson, and Adam Gerndt.

I am grateful to the many people who suggested buildings for the book and to those who, later in the process, helped scout photography and track down and review building information. In particular I want to acknowledge the contributions of Pat Hodges; Nicholas H. Holmes, Jr., Nancy Holmes, and Nicholas H. Holmes, III; the late Harvie P. Jones; Nicholas D. Davis; David Boozer; Philip A. Morris; Devereaux Bemis, John Sledge, Ann Crutcher, and Ed Hooker of the Mobile Historic Development Commission; Douglas C. Purcell of the Historic Chattahoochee Commission; Camille Bowman, Blythe Semmer, and Robert MacNealey of the Alabama Historical Commission; Robert O. Mellown; Linda and Ralph Allen; Frank Nola; David Harris; Jim Terry; Cal Munroe; Arch Winter; Patty Sexton; Nancy Reynolds Bennett; Barbara Broach; Mayor Betty

Ziglar; Major Holland; Mary Ellen Zoghby; Candace Spradley of the Alabama Council AIA; and the authors of numerous National Register nominations in the files of the Alabama Historical Commission.

The true heroes of this book are the owners and caretakers of the buildings—those who have commissioned them, restored them, and maintained and preserved them. Many of these good stewards kindly provided access for the photography and relevant information for the text. The following individuals, nonprofit groups, religious institutions, businesses, public agencies, and governing bodies deserve recognition: David Zachary Abramson, Retha J. Brannon and Dr. Lemuel Morrison, Heath and Amy Burt, Dr. and Mrs. John L. Dixon, Scott and Siobhan Gonzalez, Jeannette Bishop-Hall, Mr. and Mrs. Richard Hann, Jim and Jeane Jarrett, Austin Keith, Jr., Augustine Meaher, III, J.A. Minter, IV, Bo and Diana Osborn, Thomas S. Potts, Dr. and Mrs. Joseph B. Ray, Anne and Larry Shaw, Alexander M. Smith, Garland Cook Smith, Mr. and Mrs. H.W. Thurber, III, Beth Twente and the late Dr. Michael Twente, Mr. and Mrs. John Wallace, Willene J. Whatley, Mr. and Mrs. Danny L. Wiginton, Mrs. Frank B. Wilson, Antique Talladega/Ritz Theatre, Birmingham Landmarks/Alabama Theatre, Birmingham YMCA, Claybank Memorial Cemetery Association, Dauphin Island Property Owners Association, Gadsden Center for Cultural Arts, The Jemison-Van de Graaff Foundation, Twickenham Historic Preservation District Association, the Archdiocese of Mobile, the Episcopal Diocese of Alabama, Brown Chapel AME Church, Eufaula First United Methodist Church, Gaylesville United Methodist Church, Government Street United Methodist Church, Government Street Presbyterian Church, Green Chapel CME Church, Lebanon Chapel AME Church, Loachapoka United Methodist Church, Monastery of the Visitation,

St. Bernard Abbey, St. John's Episcopal Church, St. Paul's Lutheran Church, Sears Chapel United Methodist Church, Sixteenth Street Baptist Church, State Street AME Zion Church, Temple Emanu-El, Alabama Power Company, Bank of Brewton, Birmingham Realty Company, Mercedes-Benz, National Bank of Commerce, Reeves Peanut Company, Southern Progress Corporation, Wininger & Wininger Law Firm, Alabama Historical Commission, Birmingham Public Library, Bryce Hospital, Holtville High School, Moundville Archaeological Park, Sloss Furnaces National Historic Landmark, Talladega College, Tuskegee University, the University of Alabama, City of Birmingham, Chambers County, City of Florence, City of Huntsville, City of Lineville, City of Mobile, City of Montgomery, City of Roanoke, Town of Silverhill, State of Alabama, and all others who care for the buildings and places pictured herein.

INTRODUCTION

THIS BOOK EXPLORES THE ARCHITECTURE OF A DEEP SOUTH STATE from a particular point of view, enriched by a sense of history. The framework is the "language of architecture," set forth in ten chapters. Each chapter represents a concept that architects use to shape buildings and through which buildings speak to us—Place, Form, Space, Balance, Materials, Light, Movement, Proportion and Scale, Context, and Delight. Though they may sound abstract, if you look at buildings through the lenses of these ideas, your eye and understanding will begin to focus on how designers and builders bring the ideas to life. This approach offers a glimpse into the creativity with which architects enrich our surroundings, and a celebration of their results in the state of Alabama.

You can read this book in three ways. The first is simply to look at the pictures. Enjoy Lewis Kennedy's wonderful photography, and let the buildings speak for themselves. You can also read the short introduction to each chapter and the captions that go with the photographs, and learn more about some exceptional buildings. The third way to use this book is as a springboard. Look and read, and then visit the buildings that are open to the public. Experience these works of architecture fully, in person. And discover other places in your own community, or elsewhere in the state, that illustrate the ideas in the book. Go explore!

The approach of the book invites a few notes of caution. To begin with, a well-designed building will embody multiple architectural ideas and could aptly illustrate more than one concept, so classification in a particular chapter may sometimes seem arbitrary. By all means put the buildings in *other* chapters where *you* think they belong. As an extension of this, recognize that although the book focuses on only one concept for each building, it is the *harmonious integration of multiple concepts* that ultimately makes a work of architecture successful. An accomplished building seldom stands on a single idea.

Because this is a book of photography, we are limited to what the camera can capture and communicate. No matter the talent and skill of the photographer, some spatial complexities and organizational relationships simply cannot be recorded in a single photographic image. They must be experienced in person or, failing that, illustrated in plan and section and three-dimensional drawing. Because the book is intended for a general reader, such drawings are not included, so our focus is on what can be conveyed in photographs.

As the book has taken shape, several unanticipated themes have emerged. First is a heightened awareness of the exceptional contribution that specific building types have made to Alabama's architectural identity. Houses of worship come to mind first. You cannot see much of the state without being struck by the architectural richness that churches and synagogues give our towns and cities and rural landscapes. It is reflected in the buildings included in these pages, and in the many more that belong here but were omitted because of space limitations. They express the best of who we are and what we hope for, in a wonderful variety of forms and materials and settings. Other building types that stand out as having consistently shaped the caliber and character of our communities are the public buildings—courthouses, schools, post offices, libraries, city halls—and the buildings of local enterprise—banks, commercial and industrial establishments, early skyscrapers. They document our nature and values as surely as any statistical profile.

A second theme that emerged is highly disconcerting. It is the terrible condition of some of our architecture! We speak not just of century-old buildings in remote locations, but of some more recent buildings, as well. They are deteriorating and being lost because of poor maintenance, scarce resources, and, sometimes, a startling lack of interest. While sounding this alarm, and urging remedial action, we must at the same time salute the extraordinary dedication of the many building owners who take to heart—and pocketbook—their stewardship of our architectural treasures.

A third theme has underlying importance. It is the significance of the client and the contractor (and other members of the building team) to the work of the architect. No one said it better than Louis Sullivan, in the course of a tribute to architect Solon S. Beman, in 1915:

> It takes two to make a building. An architect alone cannot make a building. An architect is generally the instrument whereby a building is made, and, from the surface of things he appears to be the creator of it. That is only, however, the surface of things,—beneath that surface comes the impulse for the creation of things, and that impulse comes through the client. The client is interested in the character of the building. It is the client's thought that goes into the building, it is the client's thought that leads to the selection of the architect and it is this impulse and selection that brings men together and produces the result.

To Sullivan's list we must add the contractor, or builder, and the individual craftsmen and subcontractors, who transform the architect's drawings into the structures we actually see and inhabit. Their care and skill shape the final quality of a building. For buildings of any complexity, we must also recognize the role of structural, mechanical, and civil engineers and other members of the building team who contribute to a design.

Once you have immersed yourself in the photographs of this book, a final theme is inescapable. It is the contrast between the quality of the buildings pictured and the nondescript and unsightly buildings that define great stretches of the Alabama landscape. We must then ask: Do we care? What is our role in shaping the communities we live in? Are we encouraging beauty, or clutter and mediocrity? What are the decisions that affect what our communities look like and how they function?

The conclusion is brief:

Open your eyes!

Preserve the good buildings we have!

And create more!

What we surround ourselves with matters.

PLACE

And the end of all our exploring
Will be to arrive where we started
And know the place for the first time.

—T. S. Eliot, *Four Quartets*

P L A C E. Place is the most fundamental—and the most personal—of the ideas presented in this book. "To make place" is the basic architectural act: the response to a call for shelter and protection, for sanctuary, for claiming your ground. Think of tepees on the Great Plains, a cabin beside a planted field, a church steeple seen from afar. Think of an assembly of buildings in a town or city that creates a point of arrival and collecting, defining a constructed landscape of functional and aesthetic relationships. All make place in ways we readily recognize.

At the same time, *place* is defined not only physically but also emotionally. It embodies the smells and sounds and experiences that live in the recesses of our memories, shaping our identity and giving meaning to our lives. This idea of *place* is both personal and collective: The home place . . . our summer place . . . the ball field or drugstore where we spent time, growing up . . . the hardware store and bank, the church and school and filling station that mark our life together as a community. These are the settings that tell us who we are, that hold our stories and give us a sense of belonging.

Overleaf: Georgia Cottage, Mobile, 1840. *Framed by spreading limbs of live oaks, a house claims its place in nature, firmly planted at the end of a long allée. The sandy drive, dappled with light, directs approach, cutting the tension between formal white classicism and lush vegetation.* Master builder unknown. NR

Why do some buildings and sites have a sense of place and others not? What is it that makes one place differ from another in a way that we recognize and care about? The distinction traditionally has been rooted in the materials, building traditions, and responses to climate of a particular region and time: Fieldstone dwellings and stores tell of the land and life of St. Clair County, a high-ceilinged raised cottage of the Gulf Coast, a cotton gin crossroads of the Black Belt.

Other aspects of architecture also contribute to a sense of place. The use of familiar symbols—a gabled roof, a pointed spire, a crowning dome with a central clock—speaks to us in a seemingly universal language. Creative expressions of form, space, scale, and ornament make a building and our associations with it memorable. Legibility is important—a building or collection of buildings must have coherence, some sense of visual order that can be "read." And relationship is important, whether it is how the building relates to the character of its site or to the character of other buildings. Thus a chain store that looks the same in every town does not tell us where we are. It has no relationship to its setting (an enormous parking lot) or to the human scale (it is usually a big box with a big sign and little else). It has no distinctive character.

Perhaps the final quality of place is endurance. A building or collection of buildings that serve their purpose well, from generation to generation, have a sense of permanence and accumulated meaning. The longer a building has stood its ground, aging but unchanged in its essential integrity, and the more lives it has touched, if only visually, the more deeply it embodies a spirit of place.

Look around you. What are the buildings that represent *place* in your life? What distinguishes them from other buildings? What makes them special?

Every town has—or had—its main street or courthouse square, that center of

commercial life that defines the community for its residents. Broad Street in Selma

bustles still, with its corner drugstore and classic Kress five-and-dime. The buildings

have adapted to changing shopping habits without losing their distinctive architectural

character.

Broad Street, Selma, developed ca. 1870 to ca. 1930. NR

Anyone who has spent hours absorbed in the deep quiet of a library understands how intangible qualities give definition to physical places. Here, in a splendid space set aside from the busyness of daily life, surrounded by books and scenes from world literature, the reader finds a serene retreat. Gently penetrating sunlight adds to the intimacy of table lamps and aged wood furnishings, making this a place to linger.

Linn-Henley Research Library (Birmingham Public Library), Birmingham, 1927. *Miller & Martin, architect; Foster & Creighton, contractor. Ezra Winter, muralist. KPS Group, Inc., renovation architect; Son & C Contractors, Inc., renovation contractor, 1986. John Bertalan, mural restoration, 1989.*

HEBREW   GREEK   PERSIAN   ARABIAN   HINDU
DAVID   BELLEROPHON   PEGASVS   SADI   SHAHRYAR   SHAHRAZAD

Throughout rural Alabama, white frame churches mark sacred places, telling

passersby of their community's spiritual life. The wonderfully inventive builders of

this Hale County church added a three-sided porch to a traditional gable-end form.

Its bold geometry catches the eye and invites you to enter. Fortunately, the builders

left their names inscribed in a cement cornerstone.

Green Chapel CME Church, Hale County, ca. 1912. *J. A. Reece, W. G. Hardwick,*

B. L. Logan, builders.

The pungent aroma of barbecue announces the destination well before the

nondescript building comes into view. Inside it is dimly lit, unpretentious, and single-

minded—a joint devoted solely to barbecue ribs, with no frills and no extras. What

evokes place is its authentic character—an addictive blend of smell and taste,

accumulated wall decorations, and easy banter that people return for again and again.

Dreamland, Tuscaloosa, ca. 1958

For more than a century a cast-iron fountain in the heart of Montgomery has proclaimed "urban place." On the site of an artesian well, the ornate fountain transformed the colliding street grids of rival land companies into a pivotal design element, visually aligned with the steamboat landing that lay at the foot of Commerce Street and with the State Capitol at the head of Dexter Avenue. Nearby historic buildings, particularly the distinguished pair that flank the fountain (only one of which is pictured here), enrich the scene.

Court Square, Montgomery. NR. Fountain, 1885; cast by J. L. Mott Iron Works, New York. Maner Building (left of fountain), late 1860s, roofline possibly altered later. Klein & Son Building (Central Bank of Alabama, behind fountain), 1856, Stephen D. Button, Philadelphia, architect. State Capitol (far right), 1851, possibly based on design by Daniel Pratt; Barachias Holt, superintending architect; John P. Figh and James D. Randolph, principal contractors; Holmes & Holmes, restoration architect, 1977–92. NHL, NR, maintained by Alabama Historical Commission

Road and train track form the
lonely crossing, connections to the out-
side world. To folk who lived their whole
lives here, working nearby fields, the
general store, post office, seedhouses,
and cotton gin were "town." The simple
geometric shapes define a place and a
Black Belt heritage passed down from
generation to generation.

J. A. Minter & Son cotton gin,
seedhouses and store, Tyler, late nine-
teenth century

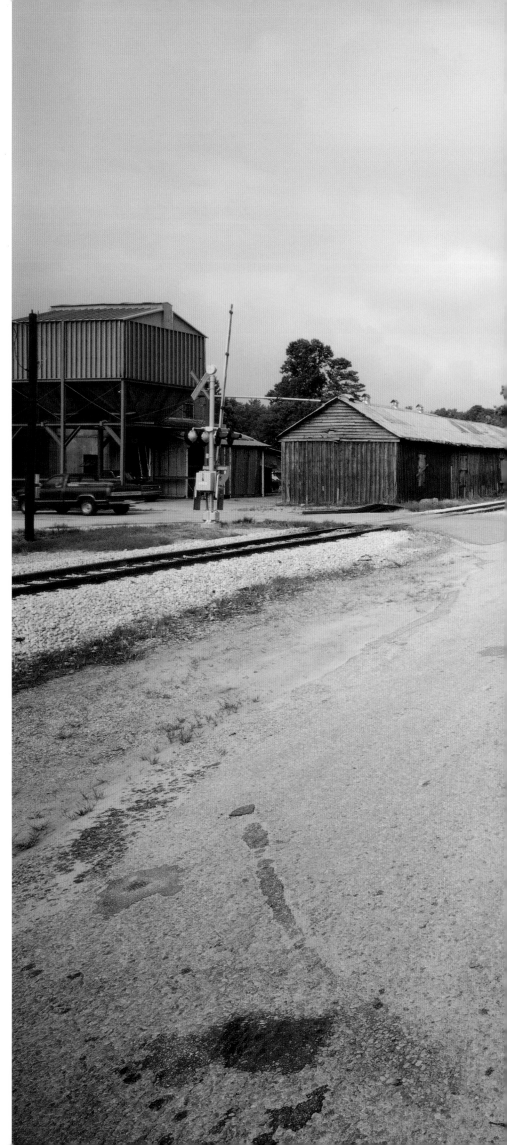

Along an isolated stretch of

road in Coosa County, an expressive

steeple rises, beacon of an ensemble that witnesses to the religious rhythms of rural

life. At the center stands Sears Chapel, with its arched memorial windows. Under

nearby trees, weathered board tables wait for dinners-on-the-grounds, physical and

social nourishment to supplement the spiritual food of Sunday services. And spreading

out beyond, toward the road, picturesque gravestones testify to the faith of generations

of local families.

Sears Chapel United Methodist Church, Coosa County, ca. 1895. *Vestibule,*

tower, and memorial windows ca. 1905.

A sheltering roof and chimneys

suggest the archetypal image of home.

Though it has suffered from weathering

and vandalism, the Asa Johnston house

retains unexpected touches of archi-

tectural refinement, including interior

wainscoting and graining and the arched

ceiling of its open central passage. The

dogtrot and the spraddle roof, which

extends to freestanding supports beyond

the porch, provided deep shade to relieve

hot summers. The house is still in the

family of its original owner.

Asa Johnston House, Conecuh County, 1842. *Ezra Plumb, carpenter builder.*

Encircling buildings create a sophisticated plaza at Five Points South in Birmingham. They stand on the points of land between five converging streets, their bending and curving facades relating to the center (once a traffic circle) and to one another. Similarities in forms and materials add to the visual unity, with Highlands United Methodist Church and the fountain in front of it providing the dominant focus. The place is full of the vitality and variety of city life, attracting nearby residents and visitors at all hours of the day and night.

Five Points South, Birmingham. *Studio Arts Building, 1994, Designform, Inc., architect; Taylor & Miree Construction, Inc., contractor. The Mill Building (Ware Building), 1930, Miller & Martin, architect. Highlands United Methodist Church, 1906–1909, P. Thornton Marye, Atlanta, architect; R. A. Stockmar, contractor; bell tower, 1921, Bem Price, architect, in association with P. Thornton Marye. Fountain, 1991, Frank Fleming, designer. Spanish stores, 1926, 1930, Miller & Martin, architect. Munger Building (not pictured), ca. 1929, Miller & Martin, architect. Urban design and public improvements, 1983, Blalock Design Associates; Mann Construction Co., contractor. NR*

Weathered in the Deep South sun, *a warehouse built in 1903 tells of a river*

town's agricultural economy. The structure's memorable twin-gabled front and ball

finials add enduring grace.

Reeves Peanut Company (Eufaula Grocery Company), Eufaula, 1903. NR

FORM

Form is a mystery which eludes definition but makes man feel good in a way quite unlike social aid.

—ALVAR AALTO, lecture to the Architects' Association of Vienna, 1955,
quoted by STANLEY ABERCROMBIE in *Architecture as Art*

F O R M. Form is the basic building block of architecture. It is often our first impression of a building—of mass defined by shape, of outlines that capture our imagination. Ancient architectural forms took their shape from their structure: Egyptian pyramids, Greek temples, Roman domes.

Their sculptural nature, in its boldness and clarity, integrity and resolution, strikes a deep chord of satisfaction. As religious and cultural monuments, they often embodied spiritual and symbolic meaning.

Form has at its core geometry—what Swiss-French architect Le Corbusier called "the language of man." For thousands of years architects and builders have used mathematics to create distinctive shapes. This is illustrated in archi-

Overleaf: National Bank of Commerce (Woodward Building), Birmingham, 1901–1902. *"Form follows function" is the well-known dictum Louis Sullivan used to describe his approach to the design of tall office buildings in the late nineteenth century. The Woodward Building exemplifies the emphasis on massing, proportion, and the expression of structure and function—rather than historical ornamentation—to achieve distinction. Its characteristic form consists of a bold two-story base with large openings for commercial display, a top section with a projecting cornice, and a plain mid-section that reflects the grid of the steel skeleton and the repetitious offices inside. As the first steel-frame skyscraper in the state, the ten-story structure signaled Birmingham's emergence as an urban center. Stone Brothers, New Orleans, architect; William C. Weston, associated architect; John Griffiths and Son, Chicago, contractor. KPS Group, Inc., renovation architect; Doster Construction Co., Inc., renovation contractor, 1984. NR*

tectural handbooks that have come down to us over many centuries, from the treatise of the Roman architect Vitruvius through the nineteenth-century builder's guides of Minard Lafever and Asher Benjamin. The drawings they contain, at once practical and aesthetic, suggest the challenge that the designer and builder must meet in creating memorable forms.

Form is at its most complex as an architectural idea in three dimensions, defining a geometry of mass and volume, often in relation to a building plan. In two dimensions, form exhibits how geometry at the hands of a skillful designer adds beauty and interest, and often graceful resolution, to a composition.

Architecture, of course, is seldom purely form. Instead, form will likely be shaped by space, revealed by light, enhanced by proportions, enlivened by movement. Moreover, a building cannot assume a form arbitrarily for form's sake alone, because architecture is layered with functional and practical considerations. It must accommodate the specific purposes for which it is built and the limits of structure and materials as well as budget. When these demands are addressed with skill, however, they can be the genesis of masterful architectural form, such as that achieved by Louis Sullivan in his landmark skyscrapers of the

late nineteenth century. Sullivan's famous statement that "form follows function" boiled down to its essence his concept that form is the creative expression of a building's purpose and structure, with ornament as an integral part of that expression. The challenge to the architect then is to find a response to functional needs that goes beyond utilitarianism and fashion to define an appropriate, imaginative, and unified form.

Look around you. What are the forms that catch your eye, that add a striking presence to your surroundings? What are the forms that enrich the landscapes and streetscapes of your life?

An ancient form signifies a dominant human presence. *More than two dozen*

of these earthen mounds lie on a bluff above the Black Warrior River, reminders that a

large, powerful prehistoric Native American community lived here long before

Europeans arrived. The temple structure is a reconstruction.

Moundville Site, Moundville Archaeological Park, Hale County, 1200–1400.
NHL, NR

Pyramid-shaped roofs make a strong formal statement *in a row of houses*

built almost a century ago for workers at the Muscoda red ore mines. Despite the

enclosure of porches, removal of chimneys, and other modifications through the years,

the dominant form continues to be a distinguishing element.

Houses (Tennessee Coal, Iron & Railroad houses), Muscoda, 1902–1903.

Charles R. and Harry B. Wheelock, architect; C. B. Ratliff, Jefferson Construction Co., contractor.

32

Massive and monumental, the Scottish Rites Temple stands in stark contrast to its surroundings. A pair of full-bosomed female sphinxes confirm the Egyptian influence of the design and act as a foil to the smooth monolithic form, distinguished by the subtle slope of its walls and prominent concave curves above the entry and at the roofline.

Scottish Rites Temple, Mobile, 1920–21. *George B. Rogers, architect.* NR

The sophisticated design for Bryce Hospital in the mid-nineteenth century reflected advanced ideas about care for the mentally ill, while relating form and massing to interior function and space. The four-story central pavilion housed the public entry, reception rooms, offices, and the superintending physician's private quarters. The handsome dome, which marks the crossing of a wide central hall on the interior, and the monumental portico added in 1884, give an imposing institutional character to the building. Flanking the main pavilion are three-story residential wings, with smaller pavilions at regular intervals.

Bryce Hospital (Alabama State Hospital for the Insane), Tuscaloosa, 1852–61, 1884. *Samuel Sloan and John S. Stewart, Philadelphia, architect; Fletcher Sloan, Philadelphia, building superintendent; Robert Jemison, Jr., lumber and brick contractor; Morris, Tasker & Co., Philadelphia, and Leach and Avery, ironwork; Alexander Baird, stonework; Kirk and Miller, carpentry. Portico addition, 1884. Numerous other enlargements and renovations.* NR

Twin cantilevered stairways in a tight two-story entrance hall create compelling geometry in the Sterrett-McWilliams House. The three-dimensional curve of the stairs contrasts with the flat rectilinear doorway, its Bohemian glass sidelights and transom tingeing the light-flooded hall red.

Sterrett-McWilliams House, Camden, 1851. *Alexander J. Bragg, possibly master builder.*

Light curvilinear forms give a lilting quality to the fanlight and sidelights of

Huntsville's Weeden House. The geometry of curves is echoed in the spiral stair and

rear wall that face the entry, as well as in the finely detailed wood trim. This

sophisticated design dates from the year Alabama became a state.

Weeden House, Huntsville, 1819. *Master builder unknown. Jones & Herrin Architects,*

restoration architect; Harvie P. Jones, restoration architect; phased, 1976–99. NR

40

Angles and arches, solids and voids compose the pleasing form of an Elmore County school. Terra cotta insets in white stucco walls add colorful geometric accents. Completed on the eve of the Great Depression, this rural school continues to serve its community with enduring style.

Holtville High School (Holtville Consolidated School), Elmore County, 1929. *PH&J, Inc., renovation architect; Lovelady Construction Corp., renovation contractor, 1983.*

41

The Broadcasting Central Building

looks like an abstract sculpture in the after-

noon sun. Against its robust curved forms,

a spiraling stair adds a decorative note as

it fulfills a functional purpose.

Broadcasting Central Building, Anniston, 1967. *S. David Boozer, architect; A. C. Martin Construction Co., contractor.*

Playing with form in a building about play, the Shelby County YMCA incorporates Ys in its entrance and bold, fragmented geometry to attract attention in its commuter-highway setting.

Birmingham YMCA, Shelby County Branch, Shelby County, 1997.
The Garrison-Barrett Group, Inc., architect; Brasfield & Gorrie, LLC, contractor.

An unexpected medieval keep in the midst of an east Alabama town, the

Lineville water tower is testimony to its designer's imagination and its builder's skill.

The concrete tower adds a touch of romanticism to a residential neighborhood.

Lineville Water Tower, Lineville, 1917. *R. T. Aderhold, College Park, Georgia, contractor. NR*

Explicit expression of its structure

gives the Cochrane-Africatown USA

Bridge a straightforward beauty. Steel

support cables, outlining silvery triangles

against the sky, are in visual tension with

the spare forms of the concrete roadway

and towers.

Cochrane-Africatown USA Bridge,
Mobile, 1991. David Volkert & Associates, Inc.,
Mobile, Carlan Consulting Group, Inc., Pensacola,
Iberinsa, SA, Madrid, consulting engineers; Harbert
International, Inc., contractor.

49

SPACE

The reality of a room was to be found in the space enclosed by the roof and walls, not in the roof and walls themselves.

—Okakura Kakuzo, *The Book of Tea*, quoted by Frank Lloyd Wright in *The Natural House*

S P A C E. If form is the basic building block of architecture, space must be its heart. It is the vital center, the most participatory of architectural ideas. We understand it best by experiencing it, by entering into it and moving through it, and by feeling how it affects us. At its finest, architectural space is not only visual but also emotional and psychological. Thus the character of a space—intimate, imposing, inviting, exciting—goes beyond engaging us to shape us, by evoking a response that arouses self-awareness and even self-potential. Frank Lloyd Wright likened the experience of space in his organic architecture to the elevated sense of self that comes from being well-dressed.

Space plays an inside-out role in architecture. It envelopes the interior purpose and function of a building in a way that shapes the exterior. Grasping this is rooted in understanding the relation between the floor plan and the three-dimensional space that rises from it, and between that interior space and the form of the building. This is what Wright had in mind when he spoke of the "within" as being the "*reality* of the building." He maintained that buildings could only be truly comprehended from within.

Overleaf: State Street AME Zion Church, Mobile, 1884, 1895–96. Scalloped circles set in scalloped braces enliven the interior space of State Street AME Zion Church. Stained glass windows echo the rhythmic patterns, which climax in the arch-framed center of worship and central window, focusing on the Word of Scripture and choir. James H. Hutchisson, architect, 1884 facade and vestibule. Watkins and Johnson, architect, 1895–96 auditorium. NR

To speak of space invokes both the idea of enclosing preexisting space and that of carving space out of a solid mass. Although it is usually defined by walls, space is not secondary to the walls. Rather, the architect consciously shapes and articulates space as volume, defining it by surfaces and screens and elements that penetrate it—by walls and columns and projecting balconies and stairs—and by openings and vistas. The progression of different kinds of spaces within a building adds vitality and interest to architecture.

Although space generally implies the interior, architecture also has an important role in shaping and defining exterior space. A sweeping porch defines an outdoor space, as do landscaping and garden walls. Urban space is defined by building facades and sidewalk treatments, by monuments and fountains and other architectural elements. The character of space is further influenced by its public or private nature, depending on its location and use. Sometimes an in-between layer of space, such as a porch, becomes a zone to relate to the world at large without quite being fully in it.

Space is the architectural place where we live and work, learn and play. We perceive it best in relation to ourselves, acting as the point of orientation in understanding its character. When a building lacks a definition of space, when it fails to heighten our self-awareness in relation to our surroundings, we are the poorer for it.

Look around you. What are the memorable spaces you have experienced? What are the spaces that add a special dimension to your life, that touch you, or inspire you, or fill you with awe?

An outdoor room in the midst of

the city, Linn Park is designed to be a

centerpiece of downtown life. Civic and

office buildings are its walls, patterned

paving defines its organization, and a

fountain and plaza at the crossing

provide the central focus. Benches and

low walls invite visitors to sit and some-

times to hear a musical performance

under the gazebo. Noontime lunches and

a host of festivals are regular fare.

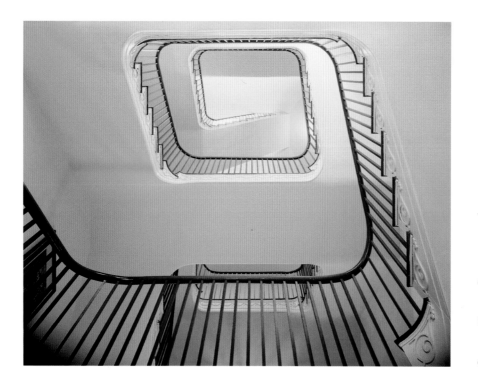

Defining space by penetrating it,

an extraordinary double staircase runs

in mirror images and climaxes in mid-

air landings. The spatial sophistication

is accompanied by refined classical woodwork, seen here along the risers and landings

of the stairs and elsewhere in door and ceiling moldings, and in a handsome Doric

entablature on the exterior.

Barton Hall, Colbert County, 1847–49. *Master builder unknown. Howard A. Griffith,*

Jr., restoration architect, 1942–47; additional restoration work, 1990s. NHL, NR

In his drawing room at Gaineswood

(right) Nathan B. Whitfield created an exceptional space. Corinthian columns and pilasters and an ornate coffered ceiling act as devices to heighten spatial awareness as well as add beauty. The pièce de résistance is the facing pair of mirrors that add the illusion of yet another spatial dimension, reverberating in reflections of receding vistas.

Gaineswood, Demopolis, ca. 1842–
61. *Nathan B. Whitfield, architect.* NHL, NR, Alabama Historical Commission property

Outdoor space is beautifully defined by the sweeping veranda of a sophisticated

Mobile house. Framed in lacy cast-iron arches, the veranda provides an outdoor room

from which to watch the activity of the street and the park beyond while remaining

somewhat screened from public view.

Chancery and Bishop's Residence, Archdiocese of Mobile (William Ketchum House), Mobile, 1860. C. T. Lernier, possibly architect. NR

Varying levels and ceiling heights shape an unexpected sequence of spaces within an economical rectangular box. From entry on the lower slope of a hill-side, where cars are parked, interior steps lead up to the high-ceilinged main level. At one end, a cantilevered sitting area with a fireplace creates an elevated nook. A continuous band of windows running along the upper walls, with ample glass below, adds to the general feeling of light and airiness.

Applebee-Shaw House, Auburn, 1954. *Paul Rudolph, architect; Lamar Brown, supervising architect; Harold Swindall, contractor.*

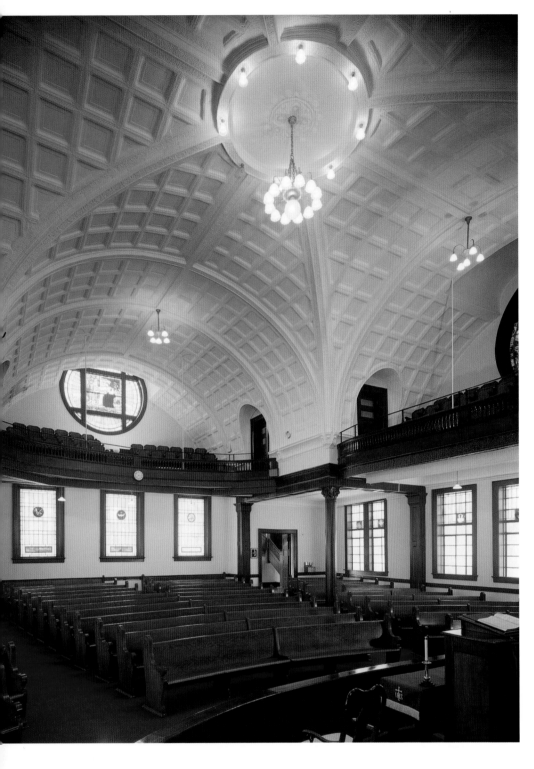

The inspiring interior space of St. John's Episcopal Church (facing page) is designed to uplift our spirits and draw us toward the altar. A series of graceful wood braces attracts our eyes upward and forward, toward the echoes of their arched forms in the opening that frames the raised chancel and in the large arched Ascension window above the altar.

St. John's Episcopal Church, Montgomery, 1855, 1869. Frank Wills and Henry Dudley, New York, architect; B. F. Randolph, builder. Chancel and stenciled ceiling added 1869. Additional renovations 1962. Stenciled ceiling restored 1983. NR

Great intersecting vaults form the majestic space of Brown Chapel AME Church in Selma. In this sacred setting, mass protest meetings for the right to vote took place and the historic Selma-to-Montgomery march of 1965 began.

Brown Chapel AME Church, Selma, 1908. A. J. Farley, builder. NHL, NR

Space is manifest from the first

moment you see the John Wallace House.

Columns define it, a serpentine staircase

carves it, and protruding balconies and

rooms accentuate it. At once classical

and contemporary, the U-shaped house,

entered on the side, embraces a central

court bordered by a long columned porch.

The house is still occupied by the owners

who commissioned its design.

John Wallace House, Athens, 1962–64. *Paul Rudolph, architect; William S. Tune, supervising architect; Cecil Black, Flanagan Lumber Co., contractor.*

BALANCE

Symmetry and Balance are forms of Order; but they are beautiful, not because they are orderly, but because they carry with them a movement and stability which are our natural delight.

—GEOFFREY SCOTT, *The Architecture of Humanism*

BALANCE. Most of us first encounter balance in the physical world when we are learning to walk, and then we test its limits playing with blocks. But the idea of balance goes beyond the mechanics of not falling down. Our natural desire for balance shapes the structures that we use to communicate ideas, including language, music, mathematics, chemistry, and physics. In the emotional and psychological realm, balance is a sign of wholeness. In architecture, balance introduces the idea of parts arranged to make a harmonious whole. This is the act of composition, and it requires both differentiation and unity.

The strictest expression of balance in architecture is symmetry, when the parts on either side of an imaginary line are exactly the same. Symmetry is especially familiar to us in classical and neoclassical architecture, in the Greek temples of the Acropolis and in many of the Greek Revival houses of the Alabama Black Belt. Both use regularly spaced columns to order their

Overleaf: No. 5 Fire Station (Washington Fire Engine Company No. 8), Mobile, 1851. With modest sophistication and great charm, this antebellum fire station shows the versatility of the Greek Revival style to serve utilitarian structures as well as monumental ones. The stacked arrangement of columns and pilasters, anchored by the plumpness of the fluted Doric columns and topped by a pedimented gable, provides a lively sense of symmetry and balance. Master builder unknown. NR

facades in relation to a center. The duplication of parts on either side of a central axis, however, is not what makes a symmetrical design successful, not what brings it to life and gives it vitality. It is rather the skill and imagination with which it is defined, in modest buildings as well as grand, with or without classical columns and moldings.

At its most integrated, symmetry will be expressed in both plan and facade, with a strong central emphasis and evenly distributed parts relating the two. The plan will likely be some variation of a wide central hall flanked by rooms of equal size. On the facade, a pronounced central element, such as a pedimented portico, or entrance pavilion, or cupola, often provides the focal point that anchors the design visually. In addition, a central dome may express a crossing of axes in the plan below it.

Symmetry may be further emphasized by an axial approach that makes the site part of the formal composition.

Balance, however, need not be symmetrical. Opposing forces held in a state of equilibrium also express balance, such as vertical balancing horizontal, or solid balancing void, or one contrasting color or texture balancing another. The greater the differences—the tension between the components—in form or shape or disposition, the more stimulating and intriguing we are likely to find the composition. And of course the architect's challenge goes beyond a creative, visually balanced composition, because it must also be structurally stable and functional for its purpose.

Look around you, through the lens of *balance*. Look for buildings that express symmetry in a distinctive, appealing way, and for asymmetrical buildings that achieve a sense of balance. Compare and contrast them to buildings that fail to express balance, that lack differentiation and "centeredness."

The magnificent Greek Revival interior of the Government Street Presbyterian Church expresses robust, three-dimensional symmetry. The balconies and deeply coffered, diagonally oriented ceiling balance the massive classical screen, which serves as a powerful backdrop for the central pulpit and communion table.

Government Street Presbyterian Church, Mobile, 1836–37. James Gallier and Charles and James Dakin, architects; Thomas S. James and R. J. Barnes, builders. March and March Architects, restoration architect; J. F. Pate Construction Co., contractor, 1976. NHL, NR

Symmetry depends on your perspective, at Kirkwood in Eutaw. The belvedere

that crowns the roof, like a miniature dwelling in the sky, is centered on the overall

form of roof and colonnade that wraps around two sides of the house. The large classical

doorways on the first and second floors are centered on the house itself, offset from

the belvedere.

Kirkwood, Eutaw, 1860. David R. Anthony, possibly master builder. Edward Vason Jones,

consulting restoration architect, 1973–79. NR

The play of horizontals and voids makes this Prairie style house a study in asymmetrical balance. The porch and primary roofs are slid apart from the center to balance each other, and the void of the porch counters the stacked strip windows of the main block. Other distinguishing features of the style, which is rare in Alabama, include the symbolic expression of shelter in the wide overhanging eaves, and the treatment of the facade as unbroken surface to emphasize the lines of the composition.

Mason House, Huntsville, 1919. J. Nathan Williams, contractor. NR

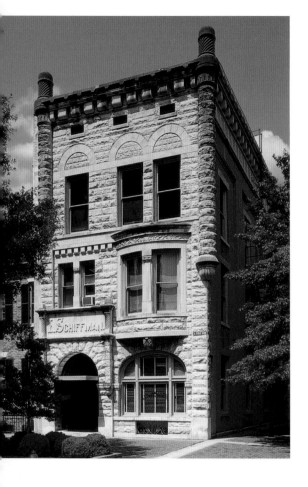

Patterns of openings and projections on the facade of the Schiffman Building find balance in their asymmetry. They stack vertically, and relate diagonally. The curve of the bowed window speaks to the curve of the entry, and the smaller paired windows hold in tension their larger twin above and the arched window below. The building's elaborate interior, once the home of a leading Huntsville real estate and mortgage company, is completely intact. Actress Tallulah Bankhead was born in an apartment in this building in 1902.

Schiffman Building, Huntsville, ca. 1845, totally remodeled, 1895. George W. Thompson, Nashville, architect; D. E. Dinnedy, Nashville, contractor, 1895. NR

Gadsden's White Palace Café *addresses symmetry and balance with an Art Moderne*

flair. Black accent bands give the composition unity by defining the center with vertical stripes

and holding in balanced tension the projecting sign at the top and the white sign band across the

building face.

White Palace Café, Gadsden, ca. 1885, refaced in enameled metal panels 1938. *Mayben & Son, contractor, 1938.* NR

Framed between stepped end gables, Wakefield uses a variety of three-part forms to express symmetry

in a highly original design. The central section is made up of a prominent pediment embracing a Palladian

window above a recessed entry. It is balanced by large flanking windows, each with its own three-part form

topped by an unusual modified triangular lintel. Other notable features of the Federal style house are its

fine brickwork, laid in a Flemish bond pattern with narrow mortar joints, and the ellipse-and-circle motif

in the sidelights of the primary windows and the doorway, repeated with somewhat heavier lines in the

addition to the left, which dates from around 1900.

Wakefield, Florence, ca. 1835. Attributed to James Sample, master builder. Dining room addition, ca. 1900. Harvie

P. Jones, consulting restoration architect; Larry Jaynes, restoration contractor, 1996–2000. NR

Built by a member of the congregation, Lebanon Chapel AME Church *represents balance with flair. The three-stage central tower squarely anchors the composition, accentuated by a fanlighted entry, louvered lancets, and a domed roof atop a bracketed cornice. Until recently the gray tones of the rock-faced concrete block facade were unpainted. Contrasting smooth-faced blocks give subtle emphasis to the round-headed openings, the building corners, and the horizontal bands at the water table and at the springing line of the arches, which order and unify the design.*

Lebanon Chapel AME Church, Fairhope, 1923. Warren B. Pearson, builder. NR

Boldly articulated towers flanking an arcaded midsection and central cupola

express the essence of symmetry and balance. A wide flight of steps rises to the deep

porch, marking entry. Above it, a broad pediment form in brick, with a blind arch that

echoes the arched openings below, holds the composition together. Sophisticated design

and construction make Sixteenth Street Baptist Church an architectural landmark as

well as a landmark in civil rights history.

Sixteenth Street Baptist Church, Birmingham, 1909–11. Wallace A. Rayfield,

architect; Windham Brothers Construction Co., contractor. NR

MATERI

Each material has its own potential, and one seeks the most eloquent expression for it.

—Paul Rudolph, quoted by Paul Heyer in *Architects on Architecture*

MATERIALS. Materials are the skeleton and skin that buildings are made of. But more than that, in the nature of the material—of the wood and stone and bricks and mortar and steel and glass—are intrinsic patterns, textures, colors, and associations.

Historically, local building materials shaped local architecture, determining its structural expression and its finished appearance. A building's character was the product of the natural materials that lay close at hand, combined with the function it served and the skill of its architect and builder. One of the intriguing discoveries about the stone temples of ancient Greece is that the forms of the columns and entablatures derived from tree trunks and lengths of timber from which they originally were constructed. The thatched roof, timber-framed dwellings that we associate with medieval England, the red brick structures of colonial

Virginia, and the adobe houses and mission churches of New Mexico all reflect the natural resources and circumstances of those places and times. Today, with strong trade and transportation networks and the scientific knowledge and technology

*Overleaf: **Wininger & Wininger Law Office (Office of D. O. Whilldin, Architect), Birmingham, 1924.** The building that D. O. Whilldin designed for his own office is a celebration of texture and color. Whilldin used rough, uneven brick to create a visually rich surface, which he accented with smooth terra cotta and a sculpted iron lantern and window guard. Robust classical leaves, beads, brackets, and a beribboned garland, molded in green and blue, stand out against the speckled buff terra cotta and variegated brick.* David O. Whilldin, architect. KPS Group, Inc., renovation architect; Brice Building Co., Inc., renovation contractor, 1982. NR

to invent new materials, we are largely free of such limitations, except in poorer economies. Unfortunately, in the process of widening our choices, we have frequently relinquished the distinct local character of our buildings.

While construction budgets must still be considered, widespread availability makes materials more likely to be used for aesthetic effect, to enhance the design concept. For example, designers in the 1930s often chose smooth terra cotta and sleek, molded metal to emphasize the curves of a building in the streamlined Moderne style. Designers of mountain lodges use rock-faced stone and rough-sawn wood along with exposed timbers to conjure up a rustic feeling.

Although architects and designers have great latitude in the materials they choose, they still must answer to Witold Rybczynski's charge that "a good architect is above all a builder; a bad architect designs first and then asks, 'How am I going to build this?'" Understanding how to build starts with understanding the nature of a given material—its strengths and weaknesses, the forms it can make, the uses to which it is suited. This understanding is epitomized in Louis Kahn's famous question asking what a brick wants to be. His answer that a brick wants to be an arch recognized that only if bricks were formed into an

arch could they span an opening and carry weight above. Frank Lloyd Wright, who had much to say about materials throughout his life, believed that the beauty of the material depended upon how well it was used by the architect.

Look around you. What buildings use materials in ways that celebrate the distinctive character of the materials and enrich your pleasure in looking at them? Find examples of patterns and textures that make a building special. Do you see buildings that miss such opportunities, that achieve nondescript results with nondescript use of materials?

Color and pattern fill the dome of the Alabama State Capitol. The vibrant painting and ornamentation seem to cascade down from the stained glass in the lantern atop the dome. Below are murals depicting scenes from Alabama history.

Alabama State Capitol Dome, Montgomery, 1851, 1906–1907, 1926–30. *Possibly based on design by Daniel Pratt; Barachias Holt, superintending architect; John P. Figh and James D. Randolph, principal contractors. Frank Lockwood, architect, interior remodeling, 1906–1907. Decorative painting and murals, Roderick MacKenzie, 1926–30. Holmes & Holmes, architect, interior restoration, 1977–92. NHL, NR, maintained by the Alabama Historical Commission*

Hewn by hand, the log Claybank

Church is representative of scores of log buildings that once dotted the Alabama landscape, a record of pioneer settlement and the pragmatic use of available materials. The few such structures that remain have often been moved, remodeled, or abandoned to deterioration in the elements. The Claybank Church takes its essential form and texture from the character of the square-hewn logs. Additional patterning comes from the notching at the corners, the split wood shingles, and the shuttered openings that provide the sole source of light, other than cracks between the logs. The church, which replaced an earlier log structure on the site, has a cemetery adjacent.

Claybank Church, Ozark, 1852. Restored 1980. NR

Bold and artful in its simplicity,

the Loachapoka United Methodist Church

turned a limited budget into a triumph.

Rough-sawn cedar is distinctively used

with thoughtful detailing to create forms

and space for worship. During late morn-

ing services, a carefully positioned win-

dow pours the sun's rays over the cross,

revealing its rugged texture.

Loachapoka United Methodist Church, Loachapoka, 1979. Nicholas D. Davis, architect; G. O. Long, contractor.

94

The designer used brick to weave pattern and color into the building fabric, highlighting a variety of arches and other decorative elements. Sayre Street School is a handsome reminder of the value the community placed on its public schools. When the surrounding residential neighborhood gave way to commercial expansion, it was splendidly adapted for offices.

Sayre Street School, Montgomery, 1891. *J. B. Worthington, contractor. Watson, Watson & Rutland, renovation architect; W. K. Upchurch Co., renovation contractor, ca. 1982. NR*

The Birmingham Realty Company

Building shows a sophisticated sense of design and materials, carried out by skilled craftsmen. Brick casts crisp shadows that highlight the rustication and taper of the pilasters framing the handsome arch. Atop the pilasters are classical details molded in deep brown terra cotta and, above the roofline, metal urns with glass globes that glow at night. The small-paned pattern of the central arched window contrasts with the smooth face of the tightly jointed brick. The successor company to the founder of the city of Birmingham has occupied this office, which it built, for almost a century.

Birmingham Realty Company Building, Birmingham, 1904–1905. William C. Weston, architect; Evans Construction Co., contractor. Giattina Fisher Aycock Architects Inc., restoration architect; Charles & Vinzant, restoration contractor, 1982.

The richly adorned Empire

Building showcases the decorative

versatility of glazed architectural terra

cotta. Architects designed the skyscraper

to be a dramatic addition to downtown

Birmingham. At the time it was built,

its sixteen stories, gleaming white with

eye-catching color accents, stood out

vividly against the city's Victorian brick

buildings and industrial soot.

Empire Building, Birmingham,

1909. *Carpenter and Blair, New York, architect; Warren & Welton, associated architect; T. C. Thompson and Sons, contractor. Renneker, Tichansky & Associates, Inc., renovation architect; Wilborn Construction Co., renovation contractor, 1983.* NR

Reflective glass and geometric purity bring understated elegance to an urban setting. The glass curtain wall floats above a black marble base, which is set back from the street to create a raised granite plaza. The building represents the rise of glass as a primary building material in the twentieth century and the minimalist influence of architect Ludwig Mies van der Rohe.

AmSouth-Sonat Tower (First National-Southern Natural Building), Birmingham, 1968–71. *Welton Becket & Associates, Houston, architect; Charles H. McCauley Associates, Inc., associated architect; The Beck Group, Dallas, contractor.*

Deft handling of wood creates

texture, pattern, and form in this classic

bungalow. Distinctive gables pair at the

front and stack on the side, with lattice

giving texture to their peaks. Projecting

rafter ends catch the light, adding a

straightforward border to the broad side

of the roof and a counterpoint to the more decorative projecting beams on the gable side.

Paired sash windows, small panes over large, are set against the fine texture of clapboard.

Duggan-Burt House, Mobile, 1912

In the Hale County countryside,

architectural students with meager

means used discarded materials to build

a chapel rich in texture and spatial

experience. Walls of old tires, packed

with rammed earth and coated with

stucco, rise out of the land to shape the

path of entry. Hovering above, the roof

of salvaged lumber and weather-rusted tin shingles sags and then rises dramatically

to open the interior to a view of the wooded hollow beyond.

Yancey Chapel, Hale County, 1995. Ruard Veltman, Thomas Tretheway, and Steven

Durden, designers and builders; D. K. Ruth, Samuel Mockbee, and Richard Hudgens, Auburn University

architectural faculty advisors.

LIGHT

The elements of architecture are light and shade, walls and space.

—LE CORBUSIER, *Towards a New Architecture*

L I G H T. God created light, in the beginning. It signifies life, creativity, divine presence. Without it, we cannot see.

In the visual realm, there is little that is quite as dramatic as the juxtaposition of light and shadow. Early Renaissance painters knew this when they mastered the technique of chiaroscuro to convey religious intensity. Rembrandt used similar techniques to evoke mystery and depth of feeling. In canvasses painted by Americans of the Hudson River School, light communicated the majesty of nature.

In architecture, the incorporation of light links the design directly to the sun. And yet it is the architecture itself that reveals the light, as Louis Kahn put it so poetically when he said, "The sun was not aware of its wonder before it struck the side of a building." Light spilling across a facade to reveal its distinguishing forms, or pouring into an interior space, brings a building to life in ways that can touch us both aesthetically and emotionally. And because the effect of the light

Overleaf: Chapel of the Sacred Heart, Visitation Monastery (Convent of the Visitation), Mobile, 1894. Streams of light penetrate the Chapel of the Sacred Heart at Mobile's Visitation Monastery, linking the richly adorned space to the sun, a daily reminder of the light of creation. Harrod and Andry, New Orleans, architect; M. T. Lewman and Co., Louisville, contractor. Hall Baumhauer Architects, P.C., restoration architect, 1991–99. John Canning Painting & Conservation Studios, paint restoration, 1999. NR

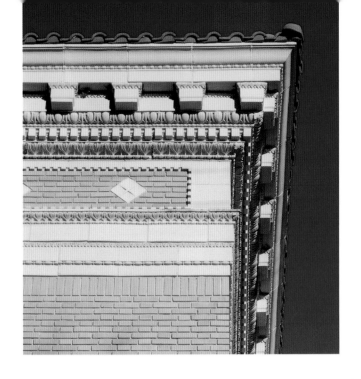

changes character from hour to hour and season to season as the light itself changes, there is a dynamic quality that is continually engaging.

How the architect forms the mass and treats and trims the surfaces to catch light and cast shadow determines how the light will play upon it, and how we will perceive it. For centuries, this manipulation of a facade's planes, textures, projections, and voids has heightened the beauty of works of architecture.

Likewise, how the architect sites and designs the building determines how the occupants will receive the light on the interior. It determines whether the welcome rays of the low winter sun will reach deep inside, and whether the interior will be shielded from the harsh summer sun by recesses and overhangs. Openings designed specifically to create special qualities of light on the interior may be in the form of carefully placed windows, skylights, or clerestories along the upper reaches of walls. We see these special effects in the light that streams down across the waiting room of Grand Central Station in New York City, injecting a timeless grandeur. And we see them in the richly colored mottled light with which stained glass windows on a western wall transform the quiet depths of a cathedral.

In this day of advanced technology, buildings can function without regard to natural light. Even when it is not considered in the design of a building, however, the sun will come, every day. So the question is one of opportunity seized or lost, to create memorable architecture.

Look for the presence of light in the buildings around you. You must be patient and follow the course of the sun. Where does it bring to life a facade you had not fully appreciated? Where does it enrich the mood of an interior space?

The rotunda of the Chambers

County Courthouse glows, as the after-

noon sun pours across the curved form

of the central balcony and of the stair

that leads to the second-floor courtroom.

Arches springing from ornamental

brackets add their own curves, defining

the circular space that marks the center

of the county's seat of government.

Chambers County Courthouse, LaFayette, 1899. Gollucke and Stewart, Atlanta, architect; M. Yeager & Son, Danville, Illinois, and Atlanta, contractor. NR

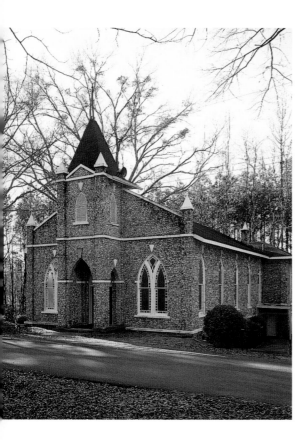

Radiant light seeps into the pristine interior of Gaylesville United Methodist Church, highlighting the patina of aged wood. The colored panes that frame the translucent glass arches add bright accents of rhythm and form. The same form is expressed in three dimensions in the vestibule through which worshipers enter.

Gaylesville United Methodist Church, Gaylesville, 1924. Church member Webb Chesnut drew the plans and superintended construction.

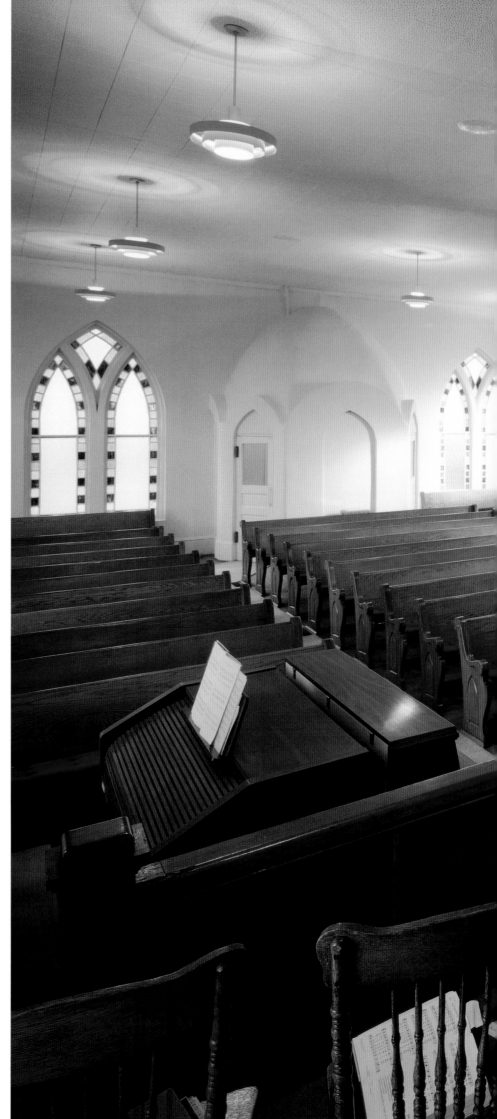

Light brings to life the handsome portico of Temple Emanu-El in Birmingham,
illuminating the planes and contours of classical moldings enriched by shadow-
sharpened ornament. On the west facade, light reveals the subtle surface texture of the
brickwork.

Temple Emanu-El, Birmingham, 1911–13. William C. Weston, architect; F. W. Mark
Construction Co., contractor. NR

Late afternoon sun catches the tips of projecting finials and the lacy trim of west-facing gables. Along the south facade, it reveals the layered board-and-batten surface, with its applied Gothic moldings. Adapted for law offices in 1964, the house continues to serve the family for whom it was built.

Keith and Keith Law Offices (Keith House), Selma, ca. 1884. NR

116

Bright light and shade give crisp definition to the Jemison House's highly detailed porch and two-tiered entry bay. Especially lovely is the filigree effect created by the shade and shadow of the insets framing the arches. The slender paired pillars and brackets that flank them add rhythmic grace to one of the finest and most innovative Italianate style houses in Alabama.

Jemison House, Tuscaloosa, 1859–62. John S. Stewart, Philadelphia, architect; Joseph Lewis, Philadelphia, building superintendent and master carpenter; William B. Robinson, Phillip Bond, New York, brick contractors. Don Buel Schuyler, architect for remodeling, 1945. Harvie P. Jones, restoration architect; James H. Fitts, associated architect; Society for the Preservation of New England Antiquities, restoration paint analysis; Guthrie Construction Co. and Triple D Construction Co., restoration contractors, 1991–2000. NR

Even stripped down to its bare cypress and brick, in preparation for extensive restoration, the Rosenbaum House exemplifies Frank Lloyd Wright's belief that light should be fully integrated into the design of a house, beginning with the sun orientation of its siting. Wright used clerestories—openings set high in the wall—as the only source of daylight on the street side of the house, while on the private side he added floor-to-ceiling glass panels to open the space completely to the out-of-doors. The bedroom wing, seen across the L-shaped terrace, enjoyed this same openness. The cut-out designs in the clerestory windows are repeated in the recessed lighting, seen over the dining alcove (illuminated) and in the ceiling along the left side of the photograph (not illuminated).

Rosenbaum House, Florence, 1939–40, 1948. *Frank Lloyd Wright, architect; Burt Goodrich and Aaron Green, construction supervisors. Frank Lloyd Wright, architect, 1948 addition. Lambert Ezell Architects, restoration architect; Eifler & Associates, Chicago, restoration consultant; B. H. Craig Construction Co., Inc., restoration contractor, 1999–.* NR

Morning light awakens the interior of the Southern Progress Building, casting dramatic shadows and revealing the textures of its native sandstone walls and granite floor. The penetration and movement of light throughout the day tie the building to nature as surely as the wooded views that surround it.

Southern Progress Building, Birmingham, 1990. Jova/Daniels/Busby, Atlanta, and KPS Group, Inc., Birmingham, architect; Robert Marvin/Howell Beach & Associates, Walterboro, S.C., landscape architect; Brice Building Co., Inc., contractor. Sculpture by Doug McLean.

120

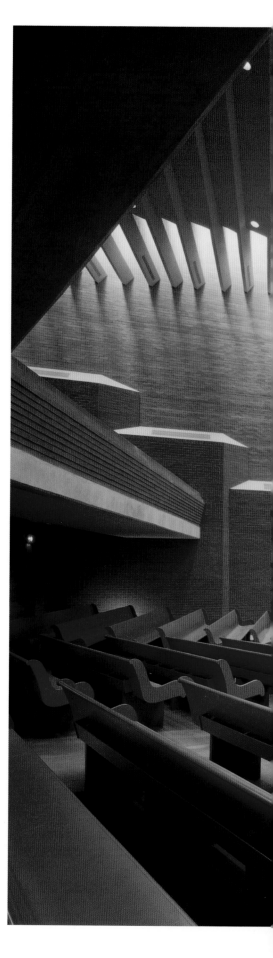

Designed to wash the sides of the nave with sunlight and set the ceiling afloat, the Tuskegee University Chapel creates an extraordinary architectural space. Two focal points resoundingly express its purpose: the pulpit, with its dramatic sounding board, and the elevated area behind (only a portion of which is pictured here), from which the Tuskegee University choir sings.

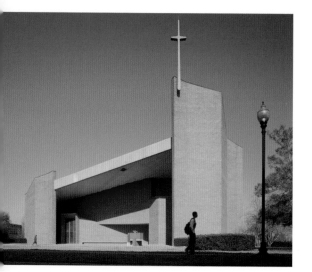

Tuskegee University Chapel, Tuskegee, 1967–69. *Louis Fry and John A. Welch, architect; Paul Rudolph, design associate; F. M. Thompson, North Carolina, contractor.*

MOVEM

ENT

Movement without motive and without climax contradicts our physical instincts.

—GEOFFREY SCOTT, *The Architecture of Humanism*

MOVEMENT. A sense of movement adds vitality and variety to a work of architecture, whether as a formal statement expressing motion or rhythm, or as a participatory event.

In the formal sense, movement has to do with flowing lines that celebrate the dynamic of curves. Three twentieth-century buildings, all of which have been pictured in the popular press, wonderfully illustrate this idea. They are the inverted spiral of Frank Lloyd Wright's Guggenheim Museum, the crowning spire of William Van Alen's Chrysler Building, and the swooping roofline of Eero Saarinen's Dulles International Airport. We also see movement embodied in the rhythmic

patterns and sequences of building parts and building decoration. For example, the arrangement of openings across a facade and the changing emphasis of major and minor elements can establish a rhythm just as in music or poetry. It may be a predictable rhythm, as symmetry tends to establish, or it may set up a more unexpected sequence, whether because of asymmetry or creative expression. Even material textures can give rhythm to the surface of a building facade.

Overleaf: Mercedes-Benz Visitor Center, Tuscaloosa County, 1997. An undulating roofline captures the excitement and sense of motion associated with Mercedes-Benz's new sport utility vehicle, first assembled at this site. Designers of the distinctive roof took inspiration from the profile of a classic coupe and the rolling terrain the vehicle was designed to handle. It is accentuated by the building's taut surfaces of aluminum, glass, and synthetic stucco. Gresham Smith & Partners, architect; Bill Harbert Construction, contractor.

The other aspect of movement is the experience itself, of entering into and moving through architectural space. Architects design building sequences to invite you to move through them, so that you will experience the space they have created. The path that leads you into a building and through it is one of the architect's great opportunities to connect with you in a memorable way. This may entail a sweeping stair that beckons you to climb. It may be tantalizing glimpses of other spaces in the distance, calling you on. Architects use an array of design techniques to lure you forward, including the manipulation of solids and voids, the sequencing of materials, the repetition of elements at given intervals, and the use of periodic penetrations of light. Perhaps the best known expression of movement is a procession of columns delineating a path that is both visual and actual.

We also see and experience movement as a design element on a larger scale, often from the vantage point of a moving car. The winding streets of a picturesque 1920s neighborhood are an example of movement created in the designed landscape. So is the arcing entrance to downtown Birmingham one experiences as the viaduct rises above the railroad tracks. A third example can be found in the patterns of circles where broad avenues converge, in such cities as Paris and Washington, D.C.

We could live in a world of buildings with no hint of movement and rhythm, but what energy and pleasure we would lose. Look around you. Do you see movement and rhythm expressed in building forms or patterned facades? Are there buildings that invite you to enter and move through them? How do they lead you on?

The procession starts at the ticket booth. A low, brightly lighted mirrored ceiling propels you forward to a two-story anteroom with exotic light fixtures and more mirrors. The ceiling drops again through a passageway, and then the main lobby opens before you, dazzling in its movie palace splendor. Clearly it is not the final destination, with its grand staircase leading upward, glimpses of other stairs going up and coming down from points unseen, and curtained doors behind ornamental gates on the main level. The restored Alabama Theatre brings to life the glamour of an earlier time.

Alabama Theatre, Birmingham, 1927. *Graven & Mayger, Chicago, architect; Thompson-Starrett Co., New York, contractor. EverGreene Painting Studios, 1998 interior restoration. NR*

A swirling stair embodies motion, epitomizing the Art Moderne style in a rare Alabama example. Hallmarks include sleek streamlined forms with rounded corners, stylized decoration, and the incorporation of aluminum and glass block. In the ceiling above the stairwell, a sky-like circle inset with a lighted moon and stars mirrors the sea of fish and waves below.

Nash-Twente House, Decatur, 1939–40. *Edwin Lancaster, architect. Phased restoration, 1980s and 90s. NR*

Rhythmic receding arches reveal the beauty of structural forms at Fort Morgan. Built to defend the entrance to Mobile Bay, the early-nineteenth-century fortification's massive brick walls were designed to protect gun positions. The rings in the floor, tracks used for positioning cannon, echo the curved forms of the vaulted ceilings.

Fort Morgan, Baldwin County, 1819–34. *Simone Bernard, military engineer, 1817 plans. Major improvements, 1896–1910. Partially restored 1930s.* NHL, NR, Alabama Historical Commission property

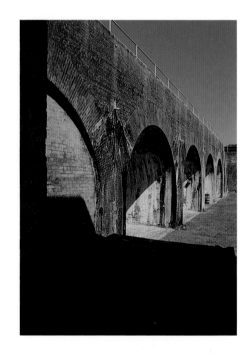

134

An embracing curve sweeps you into a composition of interlocking circles set overlooking the dunes of Dauphin Island. The

free-flowing geometry generates a sense of activity and fun, the perfect expression of a club originally built for the island's summer

home owners. Within the layers of circles are a dining room, ballroom, and lounge, as well as a circular pool and pool house. Flat

roofs and flared windows accentuate the curves.

Isle Dauphine Club, Dauphin Island, 1956. *Arch R. Winter & T. Howard Ellis, architects; Manhattan Construction Co., Texas, contractor.*

Meandering streets weave through
a park-like neighborhood, following the
natural contours of the land. The sinuous
plan, laid out in 1892 for the Montgomery
suburb of Cloverdale, features spacious
irregular lots overlooking designated park
areas, some with fountains. Typical of picturesque garden suburbs of the late nineteenth
and early twentieth centuries, Cloverdale's development was supported by a trolley
that connected it to downtown.

Cloverdale, Montgomery, laid out 1892, primary development 1910–30.

Joseph F. Johnson, possibly landscape architect. NR

A banister marks the rise and turn of a staircase at Belle Mont, an early Alabama house with strong suggestions that Thomas Jefferson influenced its design. The sunlit salon, with traces of its nineteenth-century wallpaper, is the only space on the second floor. It opens onto the upper level of the front portico, and leads by way of the hanging stair to the attic, where a rooftop observatory once overlooked plantation fields.

Belle Mont, Colbert County, ca. 1825. *Master builder unknown. Jones & Herrin Architects, restoration architect; B. H. Craig Construction Co., Inc., restoration contractor, phased starting mid-1980s.* NR, Alabama Historical Commission property

Flowing lines lead to a succession of bold, energizing curves in this Queen Anne style house. The more you study it, the more you see. The designer used other rounded elements to accentuate the curves, such as the spindlework that appears in the friezes of the second floor porch and the entrance gable on the main floor, and in the corners of the curved openings. Bulging knobs on the turned porch supports are the final touch. The irregular massing and varied surface treatment are typical of the Queen Anne style.

Shepherd House, Mobile, 1897.

Rudolph Benz, architect; J. P. Emrich, contractor.

NR

Twisting and turning, projecting and receding, a profusion of sculptured columns, niches, shells, and scrolls fills the central section of Government Street United Methodist Church (left). The highly active, lavishly ornamented doorway contrasts dramatically with the plain walls on either side, in keeping with its Spanish Baroque style. The church is a rare and notable Alabama example of the style revived in the early twentieth century.

Government Street United Methodist Church, Mobile, 1890–91, completely altered 1908. *B. D. Price, architect; W. S. Foster, contractor, 1890–91. George B. Rogers, architect, 1908.* NR

Rising toward the light, great wooden ribs curve upward, their form echoed by the ranks of the organ. They frame a vivid stained glass window that dramatically links the light above to the cross and the central altar. The integration into the design of the natural colors and textures of stone and wood adds warmth and beauty to the space.

St. Paul's Lutheran Church, Cullman, 1969–70. *Robert H. Adams of Charles H. McCauley Associates, Inc., architect; Word and Boggus Co., contractor.*

PROPORT

ION

Whoever would build so as to have their building commended . . . must build according to a justness of proportion, and this justness of proportion must be owing to art.

—LEON BATTISTA ALBERTI, *Ten Books on Architecture*

PROPORTION & SCALE. Proportion and the associated concept of scale have to do with the relationships of dimensions. *Proportion* generally refers to the way that parts relate to one another and to the whole composition, usually by means of ratios. *Scale* is most often used to mean the relationship of a building to those who view it and to the setting in which it exists.

The architect Le Corbusier maintained that harmonious proportions were the key to beautiful architecture. Such a conviction is rooted in the Greek and Roman classical orders, which defined standard building modules derived from the

Overleaf: Alabama Power Company Headquarters, Birmingham, 1925, 1951, 1957, 1985. In its old and new headquarters buildings, Alabama Power Company has given the state some of its finest urban architecture. The expressive top of the 1925 building, with its eye-catching form and colorful brick-and-tile ornamentation, reads clearly from afar. The building base is of similar scale, but it also incorporates elements that appeal to passing pedestrians—dimensions, details, and unexpected decoration not visible in this photograph. The large new headquarters building, beyond the refaced 1957 addition, relates to the original tower through scale and proportion as well as color, materials, and deferential massing. The cutouts along its top are legible in the urban skyline without overpowering its historic neighbor, and the pattern of windows helps break up vast wall surfaces and mediate the size differences between the two buildings. Warren Knight & Davis, architect; Sigmund Nesselroth, associated architect; Edward Field Sanford, Jr., sculptor; Dixie Construction Co., contractor, 1925. Jack B. Smith, architect, 1951 addition. Van Keuren, Davis & Co., architect, 1957 addition. Gresham Smith & Partners, architect; Geddes Brecher Qualls Cunningham, P.C., Philadelphia, associated architect; Doster Construction Co., Inc., contractor, 1985 addition. Gresham Smith & Partners, architect; Brasfield & Gorrie, LLC, contractor, 1987 renovation of original building.

diameter of their respective columns. During the Renaissance, renewed interest in classical architecture and mathematics led to enthusiasm for the idea that certain mathematical ratios would yield architectural perfection. One of these ratios was known as the golden mean or golden section. From a design point of view, the elements that establish a building's proportions, such as columns and moldings, are also the means of organizing the facade and enriching it visually.

Leonardo da Vinci's drawing of a male figure with outstretched arms and legs, circumscribed by a circle and a square, illustrates the idea of perfect proportions related to the human body, and introduces the human body as a reference point for scale. In the twentieth century, Le Corbusier developed his own system of proportions related to a stylized human figure,

which he used as a scale for designing everything from site plans and buildings to interior furnishings.

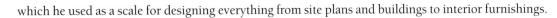

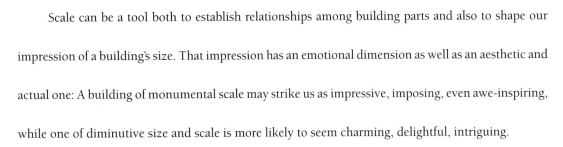

Scale can be a tool both to establish relationships among building parts and also to shape our impression of a building's size. That impression has an emotional dimension as well as an aesthetic and actual one: A building of monumental scale may strike us as impressive, imposing, even awe-inspiring, while one of diminutive size and scale is more likely to seem charming, delightful, intriguing.

Scale also refers to how a building relates to its surroundings from different vantage points. For example, for a downtown building to be perceived effectively from afar, as part of a cityscape, requires clarity of form and bold articulation. Good design requires that, at the same time, the building relate to what is frequently called a human or pedestrian scale. This calls for a finer definition of architectural elements seen up close. One of the great criticisms of modern skyscrapers of the mid- to late twentieth century is their lack of scale, particularly of pedestrian or human scale. The austere, unornamented look that was first hailed for its modernity, expressing the "up-to-dateness" of tall office towers, often in fact resulted in a kind of visual vacuum at street level, where long stretches of building bases, undifferentiated by elements of visual interest, deadened city streets.

Look around you for buildings that use proportion and scale well. How do they relate to you—the human figure—as a point of reference? How do they define and use a basic module to organize and enrich the building facade?

Two-story Corinthian columns establish a monumental scale in the Grand Gallery of the Alabama Museum of Natural History. Doors, windows, and railings whose lines are repeated in the vaulted skylight help relate the grand interior space to the dimensions of the human body.

Smith Hall, Tuscaloosa, 1907–10. *Frank Lockwood, architect; Albert Chadwick, supervising architect; B. C. Bynum Co., contractor.*

148

A handsome building based on classical principles of proportion and symmetry, Savery Library stands on the main quadrangle at Talladega College. The three-tiered cupola and pedimented central pavilion announce its importance from a distance, while the Palladian motif that frames the entrance introduces a transition to the human scale of the broken-pediment-topped doorway. In the lobby, well-known murals painted by Hale Woodruff tell the story of the Amistad revolt and portray other scenes important to Talladega College.

Savery Library, Talladega, 1937–39. *R. W. Foote, New Haven, Conn., architect; Joseph J. Fletcher, superintendent of construction.* NR

150

The grand scale of the porch wrapping around the house is the first thing you notice. It anchors the house visually, so that despite broad proportions and ample ornamentation, the house itself is almost a backdrop. Such expansiveness recalls a time when porches provided an important social setting and welcome shade in the summer heat.

Russell-Jarrett House, Eufaula, 1905. NR

Well-proportioned parts give the impression of a cottage. *A closer look, however, using the rocking chair to relate dimensions to the human frame, reveals a much grander scale. The full classical doorway illustrates how the Greek Revival style was able to integrate two dimensions: Large pilasters supporting a frieze and cornice with dentils relate by size and detail to the overall composition of the house, while slender Ionic colonnettes between the pilasters relate to the size of the door they flank and the human figure that will enter it.*

Marshall-Dixon House, Mobile, ca. 1853. *Master builder unknown.* NR

Small scale and pleasing proportions, *accented by simple jigsaw-cut porch posts and brackets, give this Mooresville cottage (below) its special charm. Originally the home of a black carpenter named Zack Simmons and his wife, Mandy, the frame cottage reflects design ideas popularized earlier in the nineteenth century by Andrew Jackson Downing, who held that modest dwellings achieved beauty through proportion and symmetry rather than by cheap imitation of elaborate ornament.*

Simmons Cottage, Mooresville, ca. 1891. *Zack Simmons, probably builder.* NR

A highly original portico with a fine sense of scale adds distinction to an older Federal style house. The designer interpreted classical principles with great freedom, truncating the pediment to accommodate a balustraded observatory and inventing a radiating sunburst motif to fill the remaining angles and decorate the frieze beneath. Refined moldings, well-proportioned columns, and reiteration of the diamond design relate the bolder addition to the more delicate, restrained facade behind it.

LeRoy Pope House, Huntsville, 1814, portico ca. 1848. *Master builder unknown, 1814. Portico attributed to George Steele, ca. 1848. North wing addition ca. 1920, Jim Myers, contractor. Jones & Herrin Architects, renovation architect, 1978–80, 1989. SKT Architects, renovation architect; Carl Lowe Construction, renovation contractor, 1999–2000. NR*

The gargantuan scale of the

Sloss Furnaces Blowing Engine Building

reflects an industrial process that dwarfed

the human figure. Rising in the center to

a height of some seventy feet, the building

still houses eight blowing engines, which

used steam power to provide the air the

blast furnaces needed for making iron.

Fresh air entered the large upper cylinders

and left through the pipe exiting the

building at the far wall. The large over-

head crane was installed during the

construction of the building.

Sloss Furnaces Blowing Engine

Building, Birmingham, 1902. Herman

Ploeger, engineer; probably constructed by Sloss-

Sheffield Steel & Iron Co. NHL, NR

The Union Station Train Shed

looms large in the distance, a reminder

of the growth of cities and rail trans-

portation in the late nineteenth century.

The long-span, trussed-roof structure

provided shelter for rail passengers

traveling to and from the city of Mont-

gomery. In the graceful gable ends,

patterns of glass introduce a smaller

scale and admit light and unexpected

touches of color to the interior of the shed.

Union Station Train Shed, Montgomery, 1898–99. *Louisville & Nashville Railroad*

Engineering Department, designer. NHL, NR

CON TEXT

Contextualism . . . means that we finally understand that history and the environment are the two faces of architecture, that no building stands alone.

—Ada Louise Huxtable, "The Troubled State of Modern Architecture," *Architectural Record*

C O N T E X T. Context has to do with the relationship between a building and its surroundings. The word comes from the Latin *contexere,* to weave together, and the concept as it applies to architecture is both physical and intellectual. A building designed in relation to its context takes into consideration the site, the surrounding buildings, and the cultural and historical traditions that affect it.

Site is broadly understood to include the entire setting, with its topography, landscape, views, and climate. Frank Lloyd Wright had this in mind when he said that no house should be *on* a hill, but should be *of* the hill, should in effect be part of the hill. Climate as a design consideration is evidenced in older build-

ings throughout Alabama, as Robert Gamble, the state's leading architectural historian, has written of so well. Wide central halls, tall floor-length windows, high ceilings, and shaded verandas give a distinctive character to antebellum dwellings while maximizing ventilation during the hot summer months. The rain porches of Baldwin County are another example of a sen-

Overleaf: Lower Commerce Street, Montgomery, late nineteenth century and early twentieth century. Individual buildings fit together with a pleasing sense of unity. While each retains its own identity, it relates to its neighbors through height and proportion, materials and window patterns, and prominent cornice. Architecture critic Paul Goldberger has said that streetscapes define cities. Lower Commerce Street defined Montgomery with great civility in the late nineteenth century and continues to do so into the twenty-first. NR

sitive response to climate evolving into an architectural form. These supplementary porch projections are a distinctive feature of houses on the eastern shore of Mobile Bay.

In architectural discussions, context most commonly refers to a building's relationship to neighboring structures. In nineteenth- and early-twentieth-century cities and towns, there was a prevailing sense of buildings fitting together, the result of available materials, typical lot sizes, familiar construction practices, and popular tastes. By the latter half of the twentieth century, however, this tendency had changed so drastically that such cities as Savannah and Mobile, seeking to protect the special character of their historic districts, wrote guidelines to help ensure that new construction would relate to existing buildings, rather than detracting from them. Such guidelines typically cite a range of design considerations, including height, scale, alignment, facade proportions, window patterns, entrances and projections, materials, colors, textures, and roof forms. One of the great architectural challenges today is to design a building that represents its own time yet truly relates to its surroundings.

What happens when buildings are designed without taking context into consideration? A building that fails to make that connection generally disrupts—and sometimes even destroys—its setting. Think of what happens when builders totally clear a wooded site rather than undergoing the trouble and expense to fit the building among the trees. Think of how it looks when the gaping hole of a parking lot interrupts a cohesive block of buildings. Think of the loss of harmony that results when the window patterns and roof forms and scale-giving elements of neighboring buildings are completely ignored. Although good contextual relationships alone do not guarantee good architecture, they do minimize negative impact. And although there are landmark buildings that transcend contextual design by their excellence, these are rare.

Look around you. Do you see buildings that relate well to their surroundings? What devices do they use? How do they compare to buildings designed with no regard to context?

165

Pansies, tulips, and morning glories are among the flowers on the ceiling of Fendall Hall's company parlor, in violin-shaped corner medallions and trailing around the border of the central section. According to family tradition, these were the flowers a traveling French artist picked on early morning walks, after being engaged to redecorate the main rooms of the house during the 1880s. Beyond the pocket doors, with their etched frosted glass outlined with ruby Bohemian glass, the dining room features a fruits-and-flowers motif.

Fendall Hall, Eufaula, ca. 1860, remodeled and redecorated 1880s. *George Whipple, possibly master builder. Monsieur LeFranc, murals and stenciling, 1880s. Ongoing restoration. NR, Alabama Historical Commission property*

When Clyde Mitchell built his
barn, he had an eye for beauty as well
as function. He gave it graceful lines and
perched it on the rise of a Blount County
hillside. Dormers and two rooftop
lanterns provide daylight on the upper
level, which is accessible from the back,
for the storage of hay. Wood for the barn
was milled on the land.

*Mitchell Farm Barn, Blount
County, ca. 1934*

Site and climate are fundamental

considerations in designing a building.

The summer cottages at Point Clear retain distinctive responses to both, dating from the nineteenth century when the porch

developed as a gathering spot to catch the prevailing southwesterly breeze and to watch for boats that brought visitors and supplies.

The rain porch, found along the eastern shore of Mobile Bay, evolved as an extension with separate supports beyond the main

porch. It gave additional shade and protection from the blowing rain of frequent summer showers.

Kuppersmith-Thurber Cottage, Point Clear, ca. 1900. NR

170

Eufaula's Vicksburg & Brunswick

Depot aligns with the tracks, its wide freight doors and fading advertisements recalling a busier time. Built by the railroads to service the transportation industry, depots had a civic presence as well, representing the identity of the town. This was a handsome building in its day, with unusual wooden brackets under the broad sheltering roof and tall arched windows gracefully defined in brick.

Vicksburg & Brunswick Depot, Eufaula, 1872. George Whipple, master builder. Metal roof replaced original wood shingles, 1960s. NR

Carrying out its commitment to enlightened use of the land, in 1971 Southern

Progress Corporation built an office building that was designed to become part of the

landscape. In essence, the building stands out by fitting in. Sensitive siting and massing,

the dematerializing effect of sunshades, reflective tinted glass, and steel oxidized to a

deep maroon-brown all relate it to its wooded site. Balconies and terraces give

occupants direct access to the outdoors.

820 Shades Creek Parkway (Southern Progress Building), Birmingham,
1971, 1993. *Jova/Daniels/Busby, Atlanta, architect; Brice Building Co., Inc., contractor. The Garrison-*
Barrett Group, Inc., architect; Bill Harbert Construction, contractor, 1993 renovation and addition.

It is hard for a convention center, designed for huge crowds of people, to fit into a city full of nineteenth-century buildings. In

Mobile, the architects used several devices to relate the building to its setting. They broke the building mass into well-scaled segments

capped by traditional gables and arches. Lightweight elements within the gables have a screenlike quality that is evocative of the city's

historical ironwork. A lighthouse-like tower gives the building great visibility on its riverside site, at the foot of Government Street.

Mobile Convention Center, Mobile, 1990. TAG/The Architects Group, Inc., Mobile, and Thompson, Ventulett, Stainback & Associates, Inc.,
Atlanta, architects; Harbert International, Inc., contractor.

A creative response to climate coupled with fine proportions and apt use of materials makes a mid-twentieth-century office building wonderfully urbane. The south-facing windows have louvers that can be adjusted to shut out Gulf Coast storms or to shade the offices from the sun's glare. At the top, premium offices open onto a balcony overlooking the city. The main lobby contains a noteworthy series of murals by Conrad Albrizio.

E. A. Roberts Building (Waterman Building), Mobile, 1947–48. *Platt Roberts, architect; J. P. Ewin, Inc., contractor.*

At its base, AmSouth-Harbert Plaza (facing page) acknowledges both the street and its neighbors, despite differences in scale. The peaked entrance and dark brown accents respond to form and color from First United Methodist Church across the street.

AmSouth-Harbert Plaza, Birmingham, 1989. *HOK/Dallas, architect; Gresham Smith & Partners, associated architect; Harbert International, Inc., contractor.*

Birmingham's Downtown YMCA is uncompromisingly modern in style yet echoes the color, materials, and massing of the 1920s school next door. Across the street is a historic church of similar dark-red brick. As the building extends away from the school, it asserts a bolder concrete-and-glass presence, somewhat screened by trees in this view.

Birmingham YMCA, Downtown Branch, Birmingham, 1983–84. *KPS Group, Inc., architect; Brasfield & Gorrie, LLC, contractor.*

DELIGHT

Well building hath three conditions:
Commoditie, Firmeness and Delight.

—Sir Henry Wotton, *The Elements of Architecture*

DELIGHT. Delight has been considered essential to good design ever since Vitruvius spoke of *utilitas, firmitas,* and *venustas* in his treatise on architecture more than two thousand years ago. During the Renaissance, Leon Battista Alberti and Andrea Palladio adapted his ideas in their own books on architecture, and finally in 1624, Sir Henry Wotton put the ideas into the English language as "commoditie, firmeness, and delight." In the twenty-first century, architects continue to cite these three fundamentals that every work of architecture should satisfy: space appropriate for the function, structural soundness, and beauty, or delight.

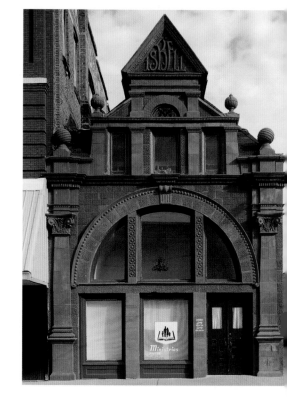

While the importance of a functional plan and a sound structure are undeniable, because the focus of this book is on the visual language of architecture rather than its practical and technical requirements, our interest here is the third principle, delight. What brings delight to a work of architecture? Beauty, certainly. Alberti maintained that the creation of beauty was almost a civic duty. "If beauty therefore is necessary in anything," he wrote in the mid-fifteenth century,

Overleaf and above right: Isbell Bank Building, Talladega, ca. 1887. An artful composition that was once the latest fashion, the Isbell Bank Building still engages passersby. Its appeal comes from its bold central arch and upward-thrusting pediment filled with stylish lettering, along with contrasting surface textures, an animated profile, and such details as sunflower tiles and the decorative ironwork in the arch at the top. *Chisolm & Green, architect; Indianapolis Terra Cotta Co., terra cotta.* NR

"it is so particularly in building, which can never be without it, without giving offence both to the skillful and the ignorant." Alberti defined beauty as "harmony of all the parts," by which he meant both proper proportion and handsome adornment integral to the design, so that each element seems essential to the whole.

But we are not limited by this historical understanding of beauty and delight. Apt use of materials that reveals their inherent qualities and reinforces the formal design concept, fine craftsmanship, or a plan that provides for function in an especially graceful and imaginative way can all contribute to architectural delight. So can the unexpected way light transforms a space, the way formal movement catches your eye and leads it on, the means by which a building is knit into its setting.

There is another dimension to delight, which has to do with romantic associations and the pleasure of playful, inventive, and even surprising design. We see this in the appeal of rambling Victorian houses full of nooks and crannies, or of stuccoed cottages with red-tile roofs that recall images of Hollywood in the 1920s. There is delight in materials used in unexpected and picturesque ways, such as twig furniture or rustic porch supports made of tree trunks that retain their bark and perhaps a few of their branches. Humor and personal references are other sources of delight. What better way to react to the horse and mule tiles around the fireplace at the Holman House in Ozark? Or the arrow-shaped balusters on the stairs of the 1830s Bishop Portier cottage in Mobile? Or the plaster head of Vulcan, god of the forge and symbol of the city of Birmingham, that architect

William Leslie Welton incorporated above the fireplace of his 1909 house? And finally, there is the delight that can come from breaking some of the rules of architectural design—if the architect can get away with it. That is to say, if it is done with sufficient skill that the building retains a creative unity.

Look around you. What are the buildings that delight you, and why? Does your community appreciate them?

Ave Maria Grotto celebrates the joy of architecture in miniature. It is the creation of Brother Joseph Zoettl, a Benedictine monk who came to Saint Bernard Abbey in 1892. Making ingenious use of found objects and materials, he built more than 125 historical and invented structures over a period of some 40 years. Among the many buildings pictured here are St. Peter's Basilica in Rome, the Colosseum, and the Leaning Tower of Pisa.

Ave Maria Grotto, Cullman, 1934–58. *Brother Joseph Zoettl, O.S.B., creator and builder.* NR

Like fine lace in its intricate detail, the highly decorated surface of the Bank of Brewton speaks of architectural elegance in a small Alabama town. Renaissance details in glazed terra cotta include flowing tendrils, vases, eagles, lion heads, dentils, acanthus leaves, and egg-and-dart and bead-and-reel moldings.

Bank of Brewton, Brewton, 1912. NR

A distinctive blend of Gothic Revival and Victorian influences come together in a charming late-nineteenth-century cottage (facing page). Slender paired columns framing pointed arches with incised decorative panels create a delightful starched crispness. The solid-faced gable of flush diagonal boards, broken by a single, low window, is lightened with a fringe of jigsaw-cut trim.

Kilduff-Ray Cottage, Mobile, 1891. *James Flandin Hutchisson II, architect; B. Sossamon, contractor.* NR

Looking almost like a child's playhouse, *the library in Silverhill has a naïve quality of delight. The peak-roofed tower juts out over the entry, supported by posts that look too narrow to hold it up. A simple series of Xs and little brackets tucked under roof overhangs are its embellishment. Recalling the building's history adds another element of delight: It first served as the land office for Swedish immigrants who came looking for opportunity in agrarian Baldwin County. Around the turn of the century it was converted to serve the community as a one-room school.*

Oscar Johnson Memorial Library (Svea Land Company Office), Silverhill, 1897. NR

190

An elephant stands watch along Roanoke's main street, whimsical reminder of an earlier time when gas stations had more individual character. When Edward Oliver Kitchens, Jr., had the service station built as a tourist attraction, it featured a tower rather than an elephant motif. After the tower was removed, however, local residents began to see the shape of an elephant in the structure that remained, and so it took on a new identity.

Gas station, Roanoke, 1930.

William Brown, Newnan, Ga., builder.

192

Quirky composition is a source of charm for Gadsden's Kyle Building. The heavy masonry second floor is held in tension by the upward pull of late Victorian decoration and the downward pull of the storefront void. The rising vertical thrust of the center adds to the sense that the building is about to take off, barely contained by the cornice cap that seems to be breaking through the triangular pediment above it. Recent restoration removed an aluminum skin that had covered most of the building for some forty years.

Kyle Building, Gadsden, 1883. *Patricia E. Sherman, Architect, restoration architect; Barclay Hayes, restoration contractor, 1997.* NR

195

Outbuildings are the utilitarian structures that make a homestead function. They are the chicken houses and smokehouses

and barns and servants quarters that are disappearing as a rural way of life undergoes tremendous change. In Eutaw, a large

storehouse and hexagonal well shelter remind us that delight can come from the workaday yard as well as from the main house.

Surely the builder took pleasure in the touches he gave them: contrasting sizes of crisscrossed slats separated by a serrated horizontal

band, arches framed in lattice, and bracketed cornices and hipped roofs topped by unexpected spires. Architectural historian Clay

Lancaster called these and a matching pair of smaller storehouses out of camera range "survivors of what must have been a goodly

collection in the region."

Pierce-Hann House outbuildings, Eutaw, probably ca. 1880. NR

Marking entry to the drive, pillars

and planters made of local stone and

seashells add delight to a Coosa County highway. Hand-lettered plaques carry the words

Villa Serena, 1917. Home of Jno. K. McEwen on Palm Street.

Villa Serena pillars, Rockford, 1917

Full of vitality and provocative rhythm, the facade of the Ritz Theatre symbolizes the popularity of movies and jazz in the 1930s. Its Art Deco design in multicolored structural glass is all the more striking because of its setting in a small-town courthouse square.

Ritz Theatre, Talladega, 1935– 36. *Timothy J. Dunn, Vitrolite Specialists, Maplewood, Mo., restoration of facade, 1998–99.* NR

A picturesque church and grave-

yard stand steeped in tranquillity. Plain

materials constructed in elegant lines

give the church enduring beauty.

St. Andrew's Episcopal Church,
Prairieville, 1853–54. *Possibly from design*
furnished by Richard Upjohn, architect. NHL, NR

MAP OF THE SITES

BALDWIN COUNTY
Fort Morgan (1)
Fairhope (2)
Lebanon Chapel AME Church
Point Clear (3)
Kuppersmith-Thurber Cottage
Silverhill (4)
Oscar Johnson Memorial
Library

BARBOUR COUNTY
Eufala (5)
Fendall Hall
Reeves Peanut Company
Russell-Jarrett House
Vicksburg & Brunswick
Depot

BLOUNT COUNTY
Mitchell Farm Barn (6)

CALHOUN COUNTY
Anniston (7)
Broadcasting Central
Building

CHAMBERS COUNTY
LaFayette (8)
Chambers County
Courthouse

CHEROKEE COUNTY
Gaylesville (9)
Gaylesville United Methodist
Church

CLAY COUNTY
Lineville (10)
Lineville Water Tower

COLBERT COUNTY
Barton Hall (11)
Belle Mont (12)

COOSA COUNTY
Sears Chapel United
Methodist Church (13)
Rockford (14)
Villa Serena pillars

CONECUH COUNTY
Asa Johnston House (15)

CULLMAN COUNTY
Cullman (16)
Ave Maria Grotto
St. Paul's Lutheran Church

DALE COUNTY
Ozark (17)
Claybank Church

DALLAS COUNTY
Selma (18)
Broad Street
Brown Chapel AME Church
Keith and Keith Law Offices
Tyler (19)
J. A. Minter & Son cotton
gin, seedhouses, and store

ELMORE COUNTY
Holtville High School (20)

ESCAMBIA COUNTY
Brewton (21)
Bank of Brewton

ETOWAH COUNTY
Gadsden (22)
Kyle Building
White Palace Café

GREENE COUNTY
Eutaw (23)
Kirkwood
Pierce-Hann House
outbuildings

HALE COUNTY
Green Chapel CME
Church (24)
Moundville Archaeological
Park (25)
Yancey Chapel (26)
Prairieville (27)
St. Andrew's Episcopal
Church

JEFFERSON COUNTY
Houses (TCI) (28)
Birmingham (29)
Alabama Power Company
Headquarters
Alabama Theatre
AmSouth-Harbert Plaza
AmSouth-Sonat Tower
Birmingham Realty Company
Building
Birmingham YMCA,
Downtown Branch
Empire Building
Five Points South
Linn-Henley Research Library
Linn Park

National Bank of Commerce
Sixteenth Street Baptist
Church
Sloss Furnaces Blowing
Engine Building
Southern Progress Building
Temple Emanu-El
Wininger & Wininger Law
Office
820 Shades Creek Parkway

LAUDERDALE COUNTY
Florence (30)
Rosenbaum House
Wakefield

LEE COUNTY
Auburn
Applebee-Shaw House (31)
Loachapoka
Loachapoka United
Methodist Church (32)

LIMESTONE COUNTY
Athens (33)
John Wallace House
Mooresville (34)
Simmons Cottage

MACON COUNTY
Tuskegee (35)
Tuskegee University Chapel

MADISON COUNTY
Huntsville (36)
Mason House
LeRoy Pope House
Schiffman Building
Weeden House

MARENGO COUNTY
Demopolis (37)
Gaineswood

MOBILE COUNTY
Mobile (38)
Chancery and Bishop's
Residence, Archdiocese
of Mobile
Chapel of the Sacred Heart,
Visitation Monastery
Cochrane-Africatown USA
Bridge
Duggan-Burt House
Georgia Cottage
Government Street
Presbyterian Church

Government Street United
Methodist Church
Kilduff-Ray Cottage
Marshall-Dixon House
Mobile Convention Center
No. 5 Fire Station
E. A. Roberts Building
Scottish Rites Temple
Shepherd House
State Street AME Zion
Church
Dauphin Island (39)
Isle Dauphine Club

MONTGOMERY COUNTY
Montgomery (40)
Alabama State Capitol
Cloverdale
Court Square
Lower Commerce Street
St. John's Episcopal Church
Sayre Street School
Union Station Train Shed

MORGAN COUNTY
Decatur (41)
Nash-Twente House

RANDOLPH COUNTY
Roanoke (42)
Elephant gas station

SHELBY COUNTY
Birmingham YMCA, Shelby
County Branch (43)

TALLADEGA COUNTY
Talladega (44)
Isbell Bank Building
Ritz Theatre
Savery Library

TUSCALOOSA COUNTY
Mercedes-Benz Visitor
Center (45)
Tuscaloosa (46)
Bryce Hospital
Dreamland
Jemison House
Smith Hall

WILCOX COUNTY
Camden (47)
Sterrett-McWilliams House

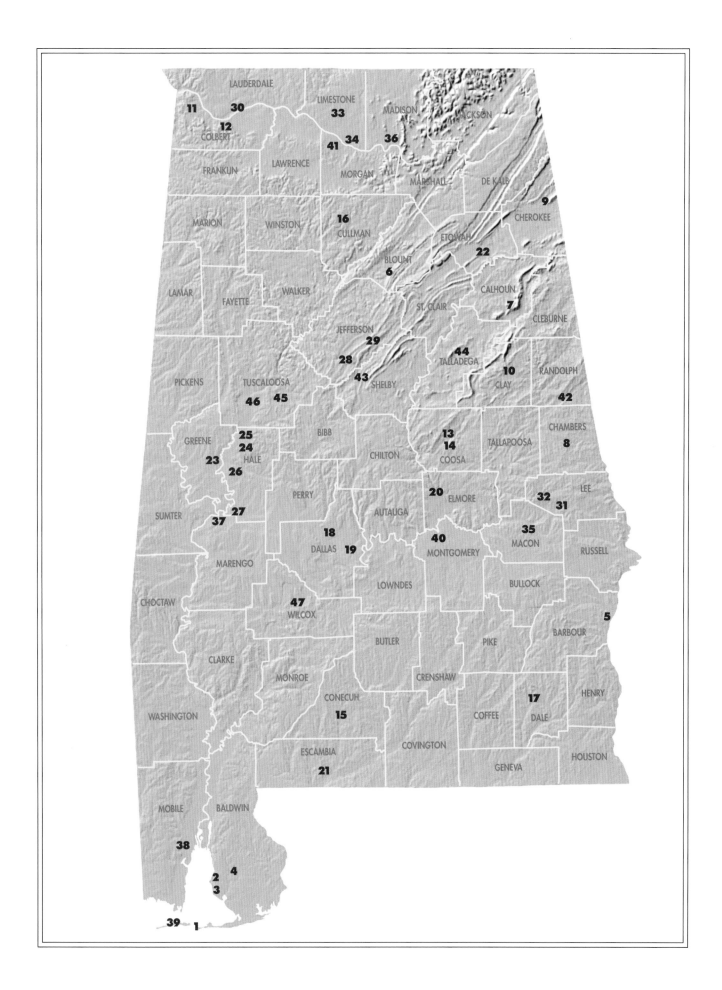

LAUDERDALE

11   30
      12
      COLBERT

LIMESTONE
33

MADISON
JACKSON

34
41   36

FRANKLIN   LAWRENCE   MORGAN   MARSHALL   DE KALB

9
CHEROKEE

MARION   WINSTON   16   CULLMAN   ETOWAH   22

BLOUNT
6

CALHOUN   7   CLEBURNE

LAMAR   FAYETTE   WALKER   ST. CLAIR

JEFFERSON
29

44
TALLADEGA   RANDOLPH

PICKENS   TUSCALOOSA   28   43   SHELBY   10   CLAY   42
46   45

25   BIBB   13   CHAMBERS
GREENE   24   14   8
23   HALE   CHILTON   COOSA   TALLAPOOSA
26

PERRY   20   ELMORE   32   LEE
SUMTER   27   AUTAUGA   31
37
18   35
DALLAS   19   40   MACON   RUSSELL
MARENGO   MONTGOMERY

47   LOWNDES   BULLOCK
WILCOX

CHOCTAW   5
BARBOUR
BUTLER   PIKE

CLARKE   MONROE   CRENSHAW   HENRY

CONECUH   17
15   COFFEE   DALE

WASHINGTON   COVINGTON
ESCAMBIA   GENEVA   HOUSTON
21

MOBILE   BALDWIN

38

2   4
3

39   1

203

SITES OPEN TO THE PUBLIC

BUILDINGS AND SITES IN THIS BOOK FALL INTO THREE CATEGORIES: those public and private properties that are in some measure open to the public, those that are not open to the public but may be viewed from public streets, and those that are on private property and are not accessible.

Only the first category is listed below, along with a few major streetscapes. For some of the buildings, access is highly restricted. For example, usually only the lobbies of office buildings are open for general visitation, and some churches are open only during worship services. In a few instances, the primary architectural interest is solely on the exterior. When possible, inquire in advance for specific information about hours, admission charges, and other requirements. Please respect the privacy and property of all owners and occupants at all times.

Baldwin County

Fort Morgan
51 Highway 180 West
Gulf Shores
334-540-7125
www.preserveala.org

Lebanon Chapel AME Church
Middle Avenue & Young Street
Fairhope
open for worship services

Oscar Johnson Memorial Library
21967 Sixth Street
Silverhill
334-945-5201

Barbour County

Fendall Hall
917 West Barbour Street
Eufaula
334-687-8469
www.preserveala.org

Chambers County

Chambers County Courthouse
2 LaFayette Street
LaFayette
334-864-4341

Cherokee County

Gaylesville United Methodist Church
355 Riverside Lane
Gaylesville
open for worship services

Colbert County

Belle Mont
1/4 mile west of U.S. 43 on Cook's Lane, about 3 miles south of the intersection of U.S. 43 and U.S. 72
Tuscumbia vicinity
256-381-5052
www.preserveala.org

Coosa County

Sears Chapel United Methodist Church
U.S. 231, north of Rockford
first Sunday in August only

Cullman County

Ave Maria Grotto
St. Bernard Abbey
1600 St. Bernard Drive, SE
Cullman
256-734-4110

St. Paul's Lutheran Church
513 Fourth Avenue SE
Cullman
256-734-3575

Dale County

Claybank Church
turn at historic marker on Alabama Highway 249
just south of intersection with U.S. 231
Ozark
334-774-2900

Dallas County

Broad Street
Selma

Brown Chapel AME Church
410 Martin Luther King Street
Selma
334-874-7897

Elmore County

Holtville High School
10425 Holtville Road
Deatsville
334-569-3034

Escambia County

Bank of Brewton
101 Belleville Avenue
Brewton
334-867-5431
interior remodeled

Etowah County

Kyle Building
Imagination Place Children's Museum
511 Broad Street
Gadsden
256-543-2787

Hale County

Moundville Archaeological Park
1 Mound State Parkway
Moundville
205-371-2234
http://shpa.ua.edu/academic/museums/moundville

Jefferson County

Alabama Power Company
Headquarters
600 North 18th Street
Birmingham
205-257-1000

Alabama Theatre
1811 3rd Avenue North
Birmingham
205-252-2262
www.alabamatheatre.com

AmSouth-Harbert Plaza
19th Street at 6th Avenue North
Birmingham

AmSouth-Sonat Tower
1900 5th Avenue North
Birmingham

Birmingham Realty Company
2118 1st Avenue North
Birmingham
205-322-7789

Birmingham YMCA, Downtown
Branch
321 21st Street North
Birmingham
205-801-9622

Empire Building
1928 1st Avenue North
Birmingham

Five Points South
intersection of 20th Street South,
11th Avenue South, and Magnolia
Avenue
Birmingham

Linn-Henley Research Library
2020 Park Place
Birmingham
205-226-3665

Linn Park
20th Street North at Park Place
Birmingham

National Bank of Commerce
1st Avenue North and 20th Street
Birmingham

Sixteenth Street Baptist Church
1530 6th Avenue North
Birmingham
205-251-9402

Sloss Furnaces Blowing Engine
Building
20 32nd Street North
Birmingham
205-324-1911
www.slossfurnaces.org

Southern Progress Building
2100 Lakeshore Drive
Birmingham
205-877-6000

Temple Emanu-El
2100 Highland Avenue
Birmingham
205-933-8037

Wininger & Wininger Law Office
517 21st Street North
Birmingham
205-322-3663

820 Shades Creek Parkway
Birmingham
205-870-8009

Lauderdale County

Rosenbaum House
601 Riverview Drive
Florence
256-760-6380

Lee County

Loachapoka United Methodist
Church
Highway 14
Loachapoka
open for worship services

Macon County

Tuskegee University Chapel
Tuskegee University
Tuskegee
334-727-8322

Madison County

Weeden House
300 Gates Avenue
Huntsville
256-536-7718

Marengo County

Gaineswood
805 South Cedar Avenue
Demopolis
334-289-4846

Mobile County

Chapel of the Sacred Heart
Visitation Monastery
2300 Spring Hill Avenue
Mobile
334-473-2321

Cochrane-Africatown USA Bridge
Bay Bridge Road at the Mobile River
Mobile

Government Street Presbyterian
Church
300 Government Street
Mobile
334-432-1749

Government Street United Methodist
Church
901 Government Street
Mobile
334-438-4714

Isle Dauphine Club
100 Orleans Drive
Dauphin Island
334-861-5255

Mobile Convention Center
1 South Water Street
Mobile
334-208-2100

Roberts Building
61 St. Joseph Street
Mobile

Scottish Rites Temple
351 St. Francis Street
Mobile
334-433-7920

State Street AME Zion Church
502 State Street
Mobile
334-438-4096

Montgomery County

Alabama State Capitol
600 Dexter Avenue
Montgomery
334-242-3750, 334-242-3935

Cloverdale neighborhood
Magnolia Avenue and environs
Montgomery

Court Square
Dexter Avenue at Montgomery and
Commerce Streets
Montgomery

Lower Commerce Street
Commerce Street between Bibb and
Water Streets
Montgomery

St. John's Episcopal Church
113 Madison Avenue
Montgomery
334-262-1937

Sayre Street School
Sayre Street at Mildred Street
Montgomery

Union Station Train Shed
behind Union Station at the foot of
Commerce Street
Montgomery

Shelby County

Birmingham YMCA, Shelby County
Branch
2610 Pelham Parkway
Pelham
205-664-9622

Talladega County

Ritz Theatre
North Court Square
Talladega
256-315-0000

Savery Library
Talladega College
Talladega
256-761-6279

Tuscaloosa County

Dreamland
5535 15th Avenue East
Tuscaloosa
205-758-8135

Jemison House
1305 Greensboro Avenue
Tuscaloosa
205-391-9200

Mercedes-Benz Visitor Center
1 Mercedes Drive
Vance
888-286-8762

Smith Hall
Alabama Museum of Natural History
University of Alabama
Tuscaloosa
205-348-9473
http://shpa.ua.edu/academic/
museums/history

GLOSSARY

Art Moderne style A consciously modern architectural style popular in the 1930s and 1940s. It has a streamlined look characterized by rounded corners, flat roofs, smooth wall finishes, bands of windows, and the use of aluminum and stainless steel. It is sometimes considered a variation of the Art Deco style, which started in the 1920s.

axis An imaginary line about which parts of a building or the main elements of a site are disposed, usually with careful attention to balanced symmetry.

baluster One of the posts that supports a handrail; a series of balusters, together with the rail they support, forms a balustrade.

belvedere A rooftop observatory.

blind arch An arch that does not contain an opening, but rather is applied to a wall surface as decoration or is set within the wall.

board and batten Walls consisting of vertical boards whose joints are covered by narrow wooden strips called battens.

brace A straight or arched diagonal support designed to strengthen the framing system of a roof.

bracket A projecting element used under cornices, eaves, balconies, or other overhangs to provide structural or visual support.

broken pediment A *pediment* that has an opening at its apex.

cantilevered A horizontal projection counterbalanced by a downward force behind a fulcrum, giving the impression of being self-supporting with one end suspended in the air.

chiaroscuro The representation of light and shadow in works of art, particularly for dramatic effect.

clerestory Windows set in the upper part of a wall to admit light; originally the upper story of a church wall pierced by banks of windows above the roofs of the side aisles.

coffered Having recessed ornamental panels in a ceiling.

colonnettes Small, slender columns.

Corinthian See *order*.

cornice The projecting ornamental molding used to crown a building or to define the meeting of wall and ceiling; in classical architecture, the uppermost projecting section of an *entablature*, often decorated with moldings and *dentils* on its lower face.

cupola A small, usually domed structure surmounting a roof.

curvilinear Characterized by curved lines.

dentils A series of small rectangular blocks frequently incorporated in the lower part of a classical *cornice*.

Doric See *order*.

dormer A window that projects through the slope of a roof.

entablature In classical architecture, the horizontal elements of an *order* that rest on the columns; it consists of the architrave (the lowest part of the entablature), the *frieze* (the middle part), and the *cornice* (the crowning part).

Federal style A restrained, refined style popular in the United States from the late eighteenth century into the early nineteenth century; characterized by delicate lines and scale, smooth walls largely unadorned except for the entrance, low *hipped* roofs, and frequent use of semicircular and elliptical forms.

finial An ornament terminating a spire or gable or another vertical element at the roofline.

Flemish bond A refined pattern of brickwork popular during the eighteenth and early nineteenth centuries, consisting of bricks laid alternately lengthwise (exposing the long side) and endwise (exposing the short side).

frieze In classical architecture, the middle section of an *entablature*; depending on the *order*, it may be a plain band or a decorated one. Also, the decorated band along the upper part of a wall or porch, immediately below the *cornice* or ceiling.

gable The triangular segment of a wall that supports the ends of a pitched roof.

Gothic Relating to the architectural style prevalent in western Europe during the Middle Ages until the advent of the Renaissance, or to subsequent revival styles derived from medieval Gothic.

Gothic Revival style A style popular in the United States in the mid-to-late nineteenth century; characterized by steeply pitched roofs, pointed arches, the decoration of projecting gable ends with curved or sawn wood trim, and the use of *board and batten* for more modest cottages and churches and of stone for more substantial structures.

Greek Revival style A neoclassical style influenced by classical Greek architecture and popular in the United States in the mid-nineteenth century; characterized by symmetry and balance, columns and *pilasters*, rectilinear lines, and a generally heavy scale expressed in *entablatures* and moldings.

hipped roof A roof with four uniformly pitched sides.

Ionic See *order.*

Italianate style A style popular in the United States in the mid-to-late nineteenth century; characterized by low-pitched roofs, overhanging eaves with decorative *brackets*, towers or rooftop *cupolas*, and the use of arcaded porches and of arched windows.

lancet A narrow pointed-arch window used in Gothic and Gothic Revival architecture.

lantern A small circular or polygonal structure with windows on all sides, crowning a roof or dome and admitting light to the interior of the structure on which it sits.

lintel The horizontal beam in a doorway or window that spans the two upright members and usually supports part of the structure above it.

massing The shape of a building considered in three-dimensional volume as opposed to silhouette or decorative elements.

order Any of several types of Greek or Roman classical columns, including their bases and *entablatures*. The primary orders are the Doric, Ionic, Corinthian, and Composite, with Greek and Roman variations, plus the Tuscan. The Greek **Doric** order is the heaviest and most massive; it is characterized by heavy fluted columns with no base, plain saucer-shaped capitals, and a bold simple *cornice*. The **Ionic** order is characterized by its scroll-like capitals (the decorative top of a column), called volutes. The **Corinthian** order is the most attenuated and richly embellished; it has a fluted column and a tall capital embellished with acanthus leaves ending in tight volutes in the four corners.

Palladian window A three-part window with a large arched central section flanked by smaller square-headed openings; a motif used by the Italian Renaissance architect Andrea Palladio and particularly associated with the *Federal style* in the United States.

pediment A wide, low-pitched *gable* surmounting the facade of a building in a classical style or above a *portico*, with the cornice molding enclosing the three sides of the triangle; any similar triangular crowning element used over doors, windows, and niches.

pilaster A shallow rectangular column or pier attached to a wall; often decorated to resemble a classical column.

portico A porch with a roof supported by columns; usually the roof is *pedimented* and the columns are classical.

Queen Anne style A visually rich and exuberant style popular in the United States in the late nineteenth century; characterized by asymmetrical composition, irregular rooflines with towers and turrets, tall ornamental chimneys, varied surface textures and materials and colors, and wrap-around porches.

rectilinear Characterized by straight lines.

rustication The use of deep beveled or recessed joints between blocks of cut stone, giving a rich and bold texture to a wall; also the simulation of such joints in another material such as brick.

section An architectural drawing that represents a building cut open by a vertical plane, so as to show the construction and reveal the manipulation of interior spaces and the relationships between interior volumes and exterior profiles that occur in that plane.

Spanish Baroque style The Baroque style, which gained ascendancy in Europe after the Renaissance and flourished in Spain in the seventeenth and part of the eighteenth centuries, was characterized by sumptuous ornament and expansive curvaceous forms. It influenced design in the Spanish colonies of the New World, as seen in Mexico and in simpler frontier missions of the Southwest United States. A revival of the Spanish Baroque style as an aspect of the Spanish Colonial style was popular in the United States in the early twentieth century.

spindlework A spindle is a turned wooden element, often used in series to form a decorative screen characteristic of Queen Anne and other late-Victorian style houses; seen especially in balusters and in the horizontal band that runs along the top of the porch and in other porch trim.

spraddle roof A roof having two pitched slopes, the lower parts of which are broken or splayed outward.

wainscoting A wall or walls with wainscot, or paneling, usually of wood and most often sheathing the lower part of a wall.

SOURCES/BIBLIOGRAPHY

Sources Cited

Sources of quotations and references cited in the Introduction and in the body of each chapter are provided below. All works and authors cited in the captions appear in the Bibliography.

INTRODUCTION—Sullivan, Louis. *Louis Sullivan: The Public Papers.* Edited by Robert Twombly. Chicago: University of Chicago Press, 1988, p. 210.

FORM—Le Corbusier. *Towards a New Architecture.* Translated by Frederick Etchells. London: Architectural Press, 1927, p. 68.

SPACE—Wright, Frank Lloyd. *Frank Lloyd Wright: Writings and Buildings.* Edited by Edgar Kaufmann and Ben Raeburn. New York: New American Library, 1974, p. 325.
—. *The Natural House.* New York: Bramhall House, 1954, p. 31.

MATERIALS—Rybczynski, Witold. *Looking Around: A Journey Through Architecture.* New York: Viking, 1992, p. 287. Wright, Frank Lloyd. *The Natural House.* New York: Bramhall House, 1954, p. 31.

LIGHT—Kahn, Louis. "Credo." Quoted in Norberg-Schulz, Christian. *Genius Loci: Towards a Phenomenology of Architecture.* New York: Rizzoli, 1979, p. 198.

CONTEXT—Wright, Frank Lloyd. *An Autobiography.* 1932. From excerpt in *Frank Lloyd Wright: Writings and Buildings.* Edited by Edgar Kaufman and Ben Raeburn. New York: New American Library, 1974, p. 173.

DELIGHT—Alberti, Leon Battista. *Ten Books on Architecture.* Translated into Italian by Cosimo Bartoli; translated into English by James Leoni. Edited by Joseph Rykwert. Reprint of 1755 ed., with "Life" from 1739 ed. London: Alec Tiranti, 1955, pp. 112–13.

Bibliography

Abercrombie, Stanley. *Architecture as Art: An Esthetic Analysis.* New York: Van Nostrand Reinhold Co., 1984.

Ackerman, James S., Peter Collins, and Alan Gowans. "Art of Architecture." 15th ed. *The New Encyclopaedia Britannica: Macropaedia.* 1981.

Alabama Properties Listed on the National Register of Historic Places. Montgomery, Ala.: Alabama Historical Commission, 1998.

Alberti, Leone Battista. *Ten Books on Architecture.* Translated into Italian by Cosimo Bartoli; translated into English by James Leoni. Edited by Joseph Rykwert. Reprint of 1755 ed., with "Life" from 1739 ed. London: Alec Tiranti, 1955.

Benjamin, Asher. *The American Builder's Companion.* 1827. Reprint of 6th ed. New York: Dover Publications, 1969.

Bennett, David. *Skyscrapers: Form & Function.* New York: Simon & Schuster, 1995.

Blake, Peter. *The Master Builders: Le Corbusier, Mies van der Rohe, Frank Lloyd Wright.* New York: W. W. Norton, 1976.

Bowsher, Alice Meriwether. *Design Review in Historic Districts: A Handbook for Virginia Review Boards.* Washington, D.C.: Preservation Press, 1978.

Bowsher, Alice Meriwether, Philip A. Morris, and Marjorie Longenecker White. *Cinderella Stories: Transformations of Historic Birmingham Buildings.* Birmingham, Ala.: Birmingham Historical Society, 1990.

Burkhardt, Ann McCorquodale. *Town Within a City: The Five Points South Neighborhood, 1880–1930.* Edited by Alice Meriwether Bowsher. Special issue of the Journal of the Birmingham Historical Society 7, nos. 3 and 4 (Nov. 1982).

"Cantilevers Create Multi-Level Interest." *Architectural Record Houses of 1956.* (Mid-May 1956): 200–201.

Clark, Roger H., and Michael Pause. *Precedents in Architecture.* New York: Van Nostrand Reinhold Co., 1985.

Connors, Joseph. *The Robie House of Frank Lloyd Wright.* Chicago: University of Chicago Press, 1984.

Downing, Andrew Jackson. *The Architecture of Country Houses, Including Designs for Cottages, Farm Houses, and Villas, with Remarks on Interiors, Furniture, and the Best Modes of Warming and Ventilating.* 1850. Reprint with new introduction by J. Stewart Johnson. New York: Dover Publications, 1969.

Fendall Hall Self-Guided Tour. Eufaula, Ala.: Alabama Historical Commission, n.d.

Fitch, James Marston. *American Building: The Historical*

Forces that Shaped It. 2nd ed., rev. & enlarged. New York: Schocken Books, 1973.

Fleming, John, Hugh Honour, and Nikolaus Pevsner. *The Penguin Dictionary of Architecture.* Harmondsworth, Middlesex, England: Penguin Books, 1966.

Fletcher, Sir Banister. *A History of Architecture on the Comparative Method.* 17th ed. Revised by R. A. Cordingley. New York: Charles Scribner's Sons, 1963.

Freeman, Allen. "Small in Everything But Quality: Loachapoka, Ala., United Methodist Church, Nicholas D. Davis, AIA." *AIA Journal.* (Mid-May 1980): 138–42.

Gamble, Robert S. *The Alabama Catalog: Historic American Buildings Survey, A Guide to the Early Architecture of the State.* University, Ala.: University of Alabama Press, 1987.

—. "Early Alabama Builders Designed for a Hot Climate." *Preservation Report* 11, no. 2 (Sept.-Oct. 1983).

Goldberger, Paul. *Buildings Against Cities: The Struggle to Make Places.* Birmingham, Ala.: Birmingham Historical Society and Harbert Corporation, 1989.

Gould, Elizabeth Barrett. *From Fort to Port: An Architectural History of Mobile, Alabama, 1711–1918.* Tuscaloosa, Ala.: University of Alabama Press, 1988.

Hale, Jonathan. *The Old Way of Seeing.* Boston: Houghton Mifflin, 1994.

Hamlin, Christopher M. *Behind the Stained Glass: A History of Sixteenth Street Baptist Church.* Birmingham, Ala.: Crane Hill Publishers, 1998.

Hamlin, Talbot Faulkner. *Greek Revival Architecture in America.* 1944. Reprint. New York: Dover Publications, 1964.

Hammond, Ralph. *Ante-Bellum Mansions of Alabama.* New York: Architectural Book Co., 1951.

Heyer, Paul. *Architects on Architecture: New Directions in America.* New York: Walker and Co., 1967.

Historic Eufaula: A Treasury of Southern Architecture, 1827–1910. Eufaula, Ala.: Eufaula Heritage Assn., 1972.

Hitchcock, Henry-Russell. *In the Nature of Materials: The Buildings of Frank Lloyd Wright, 1887–1941.* 1942. Reprint. New York: Da Capo Press, 1975.

Holmes, Nicholas H., Jr. "Vignettes of Certain Houses of Worship and their Architects." Religious Arts Festival, Independent Presbyterian Church, Birmingham, Ala., 3 Feb. 1998.

"House: by Paul Rudolph, Architect." *Arts & Architecture* 72, no. 5 (May 1955): 24–25.

Huxtable, Ada Louise. "The Troubled State of Modern Architecture." *Architectural Record* (Jan. 1981).

Jeane, D. Gregory, and Douglas Clare Purcell, eds. *The Architectural Legacy of the Lower Chattahoochee Valley in Alabama and Georgia.* University, Ala.: University of Alabama Press, 1978.

Jones, Harvie P. "The Maria Howard Weeden House: The Structure." *Historic Huntsville Quarterly of Local Architecture and Preservation* 8, no. 1 (Fall 1981): 4–18.

Knight, Vernon James, Jr. "An Archaeological Sketch of Moundville." *Native American Notebook.* Moundville Archaeological Park, Moundville, Ala., 1995.

Knopke, Harry, and Robert S. Gamble. *Silent in the Land.* Tuscaloosa. Ala.: CKM Press, 1993.

Lafever, Minard. *The Modern Builder's Guide.* 1833. Reprint, 1st ed. with three additional plates from 3rd ed. New York: Dover Publications, 1969.

Lancaster, Clay. *Eutaw: The Builders and Architecture of an Ante-Bellum Southern Town.* Eutaw, Ala.: Greene County Historical Society, 1979.

—. "Greek Revival Architecture in Alabama." *Alabama Architect* 4, no. 1 (Jan.-Feb. 1968): 6–19. Reprint by Alabama Historical Commission, 1977.

Lane, Mills. *Architecture of the Old South: Mississippi/Alabama.* New York: Beehive Press, 1989.

Le Corbusier. *Towards a New Architecture.* Translated by Frederick Etchells. London: Architectural Press, 1927.

McAlester, Virginia, and Lee McAlester. *A Field Guide to American Houses.* New York: Alfred A. Knopf, 1984.

McGee, Val L. *Claybank Memories: A History of Dale County, Alabama.* Ozark, Ala.: Dale County Historical Society, 1989.

Mellown, Robert Oliver. *Bryce Hospital Historic Structures Report.* Tuscaloosa, Ala.: Heritage Commission of Tuscaloosa County, 1990.

Moholy-Nagy, Sibyl, Gerhard Schwab, and Paul Rudolph. *The Architecture of Paul Rudolph.* New York: Praeger Publishers, 1970.

Moore, Charles, Gerald Allen, and Donlyn Lyndon. *The Place of Houses.* New York: Holt, Rinehart and Winston, 1974.

Mooresville Walking Tour. Huntsville, Ala.: Women's Guild of the Huntsville Museum of Art, 1975.

Morrison, Hugh. *Louis Sullivan: Prophet of Modern Architecture.* New York: W. W. Norton & Co., 1935.

Mumford, Lewis. *Sticks & Stones: A Study of American Architecture.* 2nd rev. ed. New York: Dover Publications, 1955.

Muskat, Beth Taylor, and Mary Ann Neeley. *The Way I Was: 1850–1930, Photographs of Montgomery and Her Central Alabama Neighbors*. Montgomery, Ala.: Landmarks Foundation of Montgomery, 1985.

Neeley, Mary Ann. *Montgomery: Capital City Corners*. Dover, N.H.: Arcadia Publishing, 1997.

Norberg-Schulz, Christian. *Genius Loci: Towards a Phenomenology of Architecture*. New York: Rizzoli, 1979.

Pevsner, Nikolaus. *An Outline of European Architecture*. Harmondsworth, Middlesex, England: Penguin Books, 1943.

Poppeliers, John C., S. Allen Chambers, Jr., and Nancy B. Schwartz. *What Style is It? A Guide to American Architecture*. Washington, D.C.: Preservation Press, National Trust for Historic Preservation, 1983.

Rasmussen, Steen Eiler. *Experiencing Architecture*. Cambridge: M.I.T. Press, 1962.

"Residence for Mr. and Mrs. John Wallace, Athens, Alabama. Paul Rudolph Architect: Vivid Restatement of Southern Neo-Classicism." *Architectural Record Houses of 1965* 137, no. 6 (Mid-May 1965): 58–61.

Roth, Leland M. *A Concise History of American Architecture*. New York: Harper & Row, Icon Editions, 1979.

—. *Understanding Architecture: Its Elements, History, and Meaning*. Boulder, Colo.: Westview Press, 1993.

Rybczynski, Witold. *Looking Around: A Journey Through Architecture*. New York: Viking, 1992.

St. John's Episcopal Church: An Illustrated History and Guided Tour. Montgomery, Ala.: St. John's Episcopal Church, 1984.

Saylor, Henry H. *Dictionary of Architecture*. New York: John Wiley & Sons, 1952.

Schnorrenberg, John M. *Remembered Past, Discovered Future: The Alabama Architecture of Warren Knight & Davis, 1906–1961*. Birmingham, Ala.: Birmingham Museum of Art, 1999.

Scott, Geoffrey. *The Architecture of Humanism: A Study in the History of Taste*. 2nd ed. 1924. New York: Doubleday, 1956.

Scully, Vincent, Jr. *Modern Architecture: The Architecture of Democracy*. New York: George Braziller, 1965.

Sledge, John S. "Mobile's Architectural Dynasty: The Hutchisson Family, 1835–1969." *Alabama Heritage*, no. 52 (Spring 1999): 6–21.

—. "Origins of the Point Clear Rain Porch." *Preservation Report* 18, no. 6 (Nov.-Dec. 1991): 3.

Smith, G. E. Kidder. *Source Book of American Architecture: 500 Notable Buildings from the 10th Century to the Present*. New York: Princeton Architectural Press, 1996.

Spaces and Places: Views of Montgomery's Built Environment. Montgomery, Ala.: Montgomery Museum of Fine Arts, 1978.

Spade, Rupert. *Paul Rudolph*. New York: Simon and Schuster, Library of Contemporary Architects, 1971.

Spencer, William M. "St. Andrew's Church, Prairieville." *Alabama Review* 14, no. 1 (Jan. 1961): 18–30.

Sullivan, Louis. *Louis Sullivan: The Public Papers*. Edited by Robert Twombly. Chicago: University of Chicago Press, 1988.

Tyng, Alexandra. *Beginnings: Louis I. Kahn's Philosophy of Architecture*. New York: John Wiley & Sons, Wiley-Interscience Publication, 1984.

Viollet-le-Duc, Eugène Emmanuel. *Discourses on Architecture*. Translated and with an introductory essay by Henry Van Brunt. Boston: James R. Osgood, 1875.

Vitruvius. *The Ten Books on Architecture*. Translated by Morris Hicky Morgan. 1914. Reprint. New York: Dover Publications, 1960.

Von Eckardt, Wolf. *A Place to Live*. New York: Delacorte Press, 1967.

Whiffen, Marcus. *American Architecture since 1780*. Cambridge, Mass.: M.I.T. Press, 1969.

White, Marjorie Longenecker. *The Birmingham District: An Industrial History and Guide*. Birmingham, Ala.: Birmingham Historical Society, First National Bank of Birmingham, Junior League of Birmingham, 1981.

White, Marjorie Longenecker, ed. Richard W. Sprague and G. Gray Plosser, Jr., architectural eds. *Downtown Birmingham: Architectural and Historical Walking Tour Guide*. Birmingham, Ala.: Birmingham Historical Society and First National Bank of Birmingham, 1977.

Whitfield, Jesse G. *Gaineswood and Other Memories*. Demopolis, Ala.: n.p., 1938.

Wilson, Eugene M. *Alabama Folk Houses*. Montgomery, Ala.: Alabama Historical Commission, 1975.

—. *A Guide to Rural Houses of Alabama*. Montgomery, Ala.: Alabama Historical Commission, 1975.

Wolfe, Suzanne Rau. *The University of Alabama: A Pictorial History*. University, Ala.: University of Alabama Press, 1983.

Wright, Frank Lloyd. *Frank Lloyd Wright: Writings and Buildings*. Edited by Edgar Kaufmann and Ben Raeburn. New York: New American Library, 1974.

—. *The Natural House*. New York: Bramhall House, 1954.

INDEX

Opening Photographs (*see index to locate additional images and information*): i, Nash-Twente House; ii-iii, Tuskegee University Chapel; iv-v, Five Points South; vi, Court Square fountain detail; x, Temple Emanu-El; xi, Empire Building; xii, Wininger & Wininger Law Office; xiii, National Bank of Commerce and Mercedes-Benz Visitor Center; xiv-1, Claybank Church detail; 2, Isbell Building; 3, Chapel of the Sacred Heart, Visitation Monastery and White Palace Café.

ABOUT THE AUTHOR

ALICE MERIWETHER BOWSHER is an architectural historian and preservationist whose books include *Design Review in Historic Districts, House Detective,* and *Town Within a City.* She serves as Alabama Advisor to the National Trust for Historic Preservation.

ABOUT THE PHOTOGRAPHER

M. LEWIS KENNEDY, JR., is a commercial photographer specializing in creating images of the built environment.